Readers' Theater

Volume Three - *20 plays*

Entrepreneurs

Author: *Lois F. Schelle Roets* Ed.D.

Topics:

Brown Paper Bag

Carnegie, Andrew

Chewing Gum Entrepreneurs

Cosmetics Entrepreneurs

Cereals. Breakfast Cereals

Deere, John

Eye Products

Game Developers

Home Remedies

Ice Cream Entrepreneurs

Inventions & Entrepreneurs

Inventions that Delight Us

Kitchen Time & Energy Savers

Mail Order Entrepreneurs

Popcorn Entrepreneurs

Refreshing Beverages

Rocky Starts - Difficult Beginnings

Salty Munchies

Taste for the Spicy

Toys

Readers' Theater

Volume Three: *Entrepreneurs*

Table of Contents

10/96

ISBN: 0-911943-43-9   © Lois F. Roets Ed.D. 1995

Leadership Publishers Inc.
Post Office Box 8358   Des Moines, Iowa 50301

Dedication

*These plays are dedicated
to my parents,
Charles & Mary Schelle,
who modeled and encouraged
entrepreneurship
and individual initiative.*

Readers' Theater offers endless opportunities for creativity to the writer(s), the readers, and the listeners (audience).

Definition & Description of Readers' Theater

Readers' Theater is a presentation or performance. The readers sit or stand at their desks or in front of the group. The script (play) is read to each other or to a group directly, or over a communication system such as public address or radio. The information is conveyed through tone of voice and manner of reading the lines.

In regular theater, there are costumes, sets, properties and actions to help the performers interpret the writer's script. Readers' theater does not use costumes or properties - unless a particular group of performers wishes to wear a hat, an article of clothing, or an object that identifies the role the reader is portraying. Identification tags may be worn or placed in front of each reader.

Readers' theater has only words to carry the story. It is up to the readers to enhance the story with expressive, interpretive reading of the lines. This enhancement is accomplished through:
  √ tone of voice,
  √ rate of speaking,
  √ emphasis of words,
  √ pauses, and
  √ response to words spoken by other readers.

How to Use this Collection of Plays

Read the plays as written to learn the information they contain.
Change them to represent other viewpoints.
Adapt them to meet your needs. *(Wide margins allow for this editing.)*
Use them as a model to write your own plays.

Who Should Use or Would Like These Scripts?

Teachers and students interested in:

  → *drama,*
  ✤ *public speaking/reading,*
  ♎ *reading classes,*
  ☆ *language arts classes,*
  ♀ *social studies classes,*
  ➡ *counselors who want to provide outlets for student ideas and emotions,*
  ♣ *Student and youth groups who need activities for meetings, weekend retreats, camping trips and related activities.*

Brown Paper Bag

Cast:

> *Historian One*
> *Historian Two*
> *Inquiring Mind One*
> *Inquiring Mind Two*
> *Stilwell*

Modifications you may wish to make:
> *Display different kinds of paper bags.*
> *Hold a contest for the best mask (or other object)*
> *made from paper bags.*

Historian One: This Readers' Theater play is about paper bags or sacks.

Historian Two: Paper bags are used for many things.

Historian One: The sack protects the object and prevents its loss.

Historian Two: The history of the paper sack or bag is interesting.

Inquiring One: What's there to know about paper bags?

Inquiring Two: Bags are bags. There's nothing more to know.

Historian One: Every item has its history.

Historian Two: In the mid 1800s, many products were shipped in large sacks or barrels. The store owner had to weigh out a pound or two - whatever the customer wanted.

Historian One: That small portion had to be put into something - a container the customer provided or a container provided by the shop keeper.

Inquiring One: I never thought about paper sacks. I thought they just always existed.

Inquiring Two:	A sack is a sack. Aren't they all the same? Besides, it doesn't take a lot of brains to figure out how a sack works.
Stilwell:	Now just a minute. My name is Charles Stilwell. I'm the owner of patent number 279,505.
Inquiring One:	What's that?
Stilwell:	That is the patent for my S.O.S. paper sack.
Inquiring Two:	An S.O.S. paper sack? I never heard of it!
Stilwell:	S.O.S. stands for "Self-Opening Sack." My S.O.S. sack had special qualities.
Inquiring One:	Like what?
Stilwell:	My design was a sack or bag that could be opened with a quick snap or flip of the wrist. It had folds that would make the sack lay flat. Flat bags take less space.
Inquiring Two:	I can see that flat sacks take up less space. It would be handy to open a sack with one hand.
Stilwell:	My sack had another quality that made it special for stores. When the sack was open, it would stand by itself. That permitted people to use their hands for packing items - not for holding the bag open.
Historian One:	The necessity for paper bags increased when stores in America became supermarkets. The supermarkets sold many items in one store.
Historian Two:	This meant that supermarkets had to find ways for customers to carry their purchases. The need for paper sacks, particularly the Stilwell design, increased.
Inquiring One:	Who else played a part in the paper bag industry?

Historian One: S. E. Pettee built a machine that would make a paper cone to carry items. He licensed companies to use his design. He collected royalties on these machines.

Historian Two: Pettee's success at making money on a device to form paper into containers spurred other inventors and entrepreneurs to improve paper carriers - that is, paper bags and sacks.

Historian One: The Union Bag and Paper company produced 606 million bags in its first year. That was 1875.

Inquiring One: Are inventors working on new designs?

Historian Two: As long the paper bag is so useful, and there is money to be made, inventors and entrepreneurs will come up with new ideas.

Inquiring Two: Maybe someday I'll invent something.

Historians One: Do it.

Historian Two: We'll be waiting to report your achievements.

The End

Andrew Carnegie

Cast
Narrator One
Narrator Two
Andrew Carnegie

Modifications you may wish to make
If your community has a Carnegie library, visit that library.

One: Andrew Carnegie is the subject of today's play.

Two: Andrew Carnegie is a person who came from poor beginnings, made enormous amounts of money in the steel industry, and helped many people with that money.

Carnegie: I was born in Scotland in 1835. I came to America when I was 12 years old.

One: Before coming to America, he received regular schooling in Scotland. His father wove cloth by hand.

Two: After steam machinery for weaving came into use, his father sold his hand looms and household goods and came to America with his wife and two sons.

Carnegie: We settled in Allegheny City, a suburb of Pittsburgh, Pennsylvania. Relatives had previously moved to the area. We were among loved ones.

One: Young Andrew and his father worked in a cotton factory.

Two: His mother made a little money by binding shoes at home.

Carnegie: When I was 15, I became a telegraph messenger boy. By 17, I was a telegraph operator. My next job was as railroad clerk for the Pennsylvania Railroad.

One: Next, Carnegie became a train dispatcher. By the time he was 24 years old, he was a division manager.

Two: He had also invested money in the Woodruff Sleeping Car Company - the successful forerunner of the Pullman Company. Because the railroads were growing, these investments earned money.

Carnegie: During the Civil War, I organized the telegraph department of the Union Army. It was also during the Civil War, 1864, that I entered the iron business.

One: In 1873, Carnegie saw a demonstration on the Bessemer process of making steel.

Carnegie: I saw immediately that steel was a stronger, more versatile product than was iron. I founded the Carnegie Steel Company.

Two: Carnegie's steel company was a large and successful enterprise. It was eventually sold to the United Steel Corporation.

Carnegie: When I retired, I was very wealthy. I made that money by hard work, foresight, and wise investments. I wanted to apply my special skills and money to help the people.

One: He spent much of his time and money to support education, public libraries, and world peace. He wrote several books.

Two: Andrew Carnegie left many of his millions to causes in which he believed.

One: The Carnegie Corporation of New York has an endowment of 135 million dollars. Grants are made primarily to colleges, universities, and educational institutions, and to organizations that conduct research in education and public affairs.

Carnegie: The Carnegie Endowment for International Peace is an organization I founded to promote peace and understanding among nations. The Endowment conducts programs of research, discussion, publication and education, in international affairs and United States foreign policy.

One: Carnegie Foundation for the Advancement of Teaching is an organization that promotes the dignity of the teaching profession and the cause of higher education. It has an endowment of 15 million dollars.

Two: The Carnegie Hero Fund Commission is a foundation that awards medals to persons who heroically save, or attempt to save, the lives of others.

Carnegie: I am happy that my money is put to good use. Of all the causes I supported, the cause of free public libraries is my favorite.

One: Free public libraries were built with money given by Carnegie. During his lifetime, he gave over $56 million to build more than 2,500 libraries in English speaking countries - 1700 of them are in the United States.

Carnegie: I donated the buildings on the condition that the communities in which the libraries were located would supply and support the libraries. My gifts were never a free handout. They required something from the recipient.

Two: The last library grant for a building was given in 1917. Since his death, the Carnegie Corporation of New York has given more than $13 million in grants to libraries.

Carnegie: My life was from humble Scottish beginnings. It flourished in America - the land of opportunities. I seized each opportunity and made the most of it. I advise you to do the same.

The End

Breakfast   Cereals

Cast
  Eater One
  Eater Two
  Narrator
  Historian

Modifications you may wish to make:
  Add information on other cereals.
  Bring the box (empty or full) of your favorite cereal.
    Be ready to state which grains are in the cereal.
Brand names and/or registered trademarks referenced in this play are:
Cream of Wheat, Grapenuts, Quaker Oats

Narrator: Our play opens today at the breakfast table.
Two people - we'll call them "Eaters" - are eating cereal.

One: I like this cereal. It is warm and makes me feel good.

Two: What are you eating?

One: Cream of Wheat. My dad and my grandpa eat Cream of Wheat.

Narrator: Cream of Wheat was first packaged by Tom Amidon, a
partner in a flour mill. Amidon's wife had been cooking the
wheat berry for him and their children. His family liked it.

Historian: The mill regularly ground wheat into flour.
But now sales were slow. Something had to be
done to improve sales. Amidon decided to package
the wheat berry and sell it as a cereal.

Narrator: Amidon reasoned that if his family liked it, so would others.

Historian: Samples of the wheat berry cereal were packaged in boxes
made from scrap paper. Samples were sent to merchants.
The product, Cream of Wheat, sold very quickly. Soon,
dealers were ordering huge quantities of Cream of Wheat.

One: My dad says that Cream of Wheat makes him strong.

Two: My favorite wheat cereal is Grapenuts. I read on the box that there is wheat and barley in Grapenuts.

One: Our teacher said that most cereals are made up of one or more of the basic cereal grains: corn, oats, rice or wheat.

Two: My Aunt Sadie works at the Quaker Oats company in Cedar Rapids, Iowa. They make oatmeal - tons of oatmeal.

Narrator: Cereals can be classified in several ways.

Historian: They can be classified by the type of grain used. Barley, corn, oats, rice and wheat are often used.

Narrator: They can also be classified as hot or cold. And hot cereals can be further classified as instant, quick-cooking, or regular.

One: We always have packages of instant oatmeal. My mom buys the regular and flavored. Apple cinnamon is my favorite.

Two: Our teacher told us that grains are good for us.

Historian: A German immigrant, Ferdinand Schumacher, helped to make oatmeal popular in this country. He invented a machine that would would roll and cut the wheat. This made it cook faster.

Narrator: Grains, and the cereals made from them, provide us with long-term energy.

One: Do you like cereal with things added?

Two: You mean like nuts, fruits, honey, marshmallows?

One: Yes.

Two: Sometimes I like them, but most of the time I don't.

One: Same here. Sometimes I like different flavors but when I'm really hungry, I like just plain cereal - a big bowl for breakfast, for lunch, or even supper.

Two: Our family eats a bowl of cereal before we go to bed.

One: All the time?

Two: No, not all the time but lots of times. My mom
          says we can eat a bowl of cereal anytime we want.
          We're a busy family and she doesn't want us to go
          hungry or eat lots of junk food.

Narrator: Cereals made from grains have been around for as
          long as history has been recorded. They have been
          rolled, puffed, baked, boiled, and exploded.

Historian: Cereals are eaten plain or with other things added.
          My favorite cereal is _____ (cereal name).
          It is made of _____ (name the grain/grains).

          ----optional insert----
          Audience recites - if the audience has come prepared.
          Follow this pattern:
          My favorite cereal is _____ (cereal name).
          It is made of _____ (name the grain/grains).

One: Cereals are good to eat and good for us.

Two: They make us strong. And sometimes, the
          boxes even have a prize in them.

Historian: And so the popularity of cereals continues to grow.

Narrator: As our lifestyles become busier, many more cereals
          will become available. Many more boxes of cereal
          will be eaten by many more people.

Historian: Will you, in the audience, be the one to develop
          and market our next best-selling cereal?

One&Two: We'll see.

All: Good-bye.   *The End*

Chewing Gum

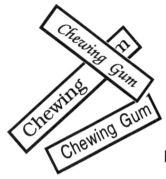

Cast
> Gum Chewer One
> Gum Chewer Two
> Historian
> Gum Expert

Modifications you may wish to make:
> *Conduct an opinion poll about favorite gum.*

Brand names and/or registered trademarks referenced in this play
include: Fleer Bubble Gum, Black Jack, Chiclets and Wrigley's.

One: I always have gum in my pocket. I chew
it when I am thirsty, tense, or relaxing.

Two: I like the sugarless. Then I don't have to
worry about too much sugar or sugar
staying on my teeth.

Historian: The "chewing part" of gum is chicle, the dried
sap of a Central American tree, the sapodilla.

Expert: Chemists tried to make artificial rubber
from chicle. That didn't work. Santa Anna,
the Mexican general, enjoyed chewing chicle.

Historian: The first chewing gum products were balls and
long strips. It took considerable effort to chew it.

Expert: Thomas Adams of New York was one
of the first to sell gum.

One: Who made cinnamon gum and all the other flavors?

Historian: John Colgan, a druggist from Louisville, Kentucky,
added flavoring to the gum. Thomas Adams followed suit.

Two: What was the first flavor?

Expert: The first flavor was licorice. It was called
Black Jack and is still marketed today.

One: I chew bubble gum.

Historian: Frank and Henry Fleer developed bubble gum. Trial-and-error perfected the product. At first the product stuck to the face and was too wet.

One: They must have worked out the problems because bubble gum is just right.

Two: My mom carries Chiclets in her purse. She likes the combination of candy and gum.

Historian: Gum with the candy coating was developed by Frank and Henry Fleer - the same developers who produced bubble gum.

Expert: The person who made his fortune in gum is William Wrigley, Jr. He successfully marketed gum to candy stores and other places that would buy from him.

Historian: Wrigley gave premiums - free gifts. He was a tireless worker who traveled extensively.

Expert: In 1892, Wrigley introduced Spearmint and within a year Juicy Fruit was available.

Historian: By 1921, he was selling 8.5 million dollars worth of gum. With top advertising strategies, chewing gum was available to everyone.

One: Wrigley Field in Chicago is named after him. Wrigley Field, gum, and baseball - that's a good combination.

Two: I suppose you could say that Wrigley Field is the baseball field that gum built.

Historian: Think about the entrepreneurs and the gum industry the next time you are at Wrigley's Field in Chicago, or see it on television.

The End

Cosmetic Entrepreneurs

Cast

Chorus - (if possible, males and females). Chorus represents the desire for all people to look their best.
D.H. McConnell
Helena Rubenstein
Historian
Madame C.J. Walker
Mary Kay Ash
Max Factor
Narrator One
Narrator Two

Modifications you may wish to make:
Add items or interviews of local interest.
Divide this play into several shorter plays.

Brand names and/or registered trademarks referenced in this play include:
Avon, Mary Kay Cosmetics, Max Factor, Helena Rubenstein.

<u>Narrator One:</u>	Audience, your attention is suggested As we tell about cosmetics - a topic you requested.
<u>Chorus:</u>	Make me beautiful; make me look great. No trial-and-error approach; nothing to translate.
<u>Narrator Two:</u>	People for generations and generations have wanted to look beautiful.
<u>Narrator One:</u>	And yet, beauty is in the eyes of the beholder. And that beholder is ourselves and others.
<u>Chorus:</u>	Make me beautiful; make me look great. No trial-and-error approach; nothing to translate.
<u>Narrator Two:</u>	Permit me to introduce our guests of honor. *(motions to each as each is introduced).* Helena Rubenstein, founder of Helena Rubenstein Cosmetics.
<u>Rubenstein:</u>	*(Nods to audience.)*
<u>Narrator Two:</u>	D.H. McConnell, the founder of Avon products.

McConnell:	*(Nods to audience.)*
Narrator Two:	Madame C.J. Walker, founder of cosmetics especially designed for black women.
Walker:	*(nods to audience)*
Narrator Two:	Mary Kay Ash, founder of Mary Kay Cosmetics.
Ash:	*(nods to audience).*
Chorus:	Make me beautiful; make me look great. No trial-and-error; nothing to translate.
Historian:	Helena Rubinstein lived from 1870-1965. She was a daughter of a middle-class Polish-Jewish merchant from Krakow. She became one of the world's wealthiest businesswomen.
Rubenstein:	At 18, I left home for Australia. In Melbourne, I opened a beauty salon.
Narrator One:	Was the business a success?
Narrator Two:	Did a lot of people come to be made beautiful?
Rubenstein:	Of course they came. My beauty products helped to bring out the best in people. I helped them look and feel beautiful.
Historian:	A short time later, Helena Rubenstein left Australia. She used the profits from the Australian venture to launch a European business.
Rubinstein:	By 1918, I had salons in Europe and the United States. My products and advice were valued by all who wanted to look their best.
Narrator One:	Did you continue to open more beauty shops?

Rubenstein:	No. A successful entrepreneur must always be looking for better ways to market a product. Sometimes that means continuing to do what you have done. At other times, you must think of new marketing plans.
Narrator Two:	What was your new marketing plan?
Rubenstein:	Instead of opening more of my own shops, I contracted with department stores to sell my products.
Narrator One:	Is this a good marketing plan?
Rubenstein:	Yes. The department store owns or rents the building We agree on wholesale prices. The department store buys at wholesale prices and sells at retail prices.
Narrator Two:	What are wholesale and retail prices?
Rubenstein:	That's a good question. Retail prices are prices you, the general public, pay for a product. Wholesale price are cheaper prices the dealer pays. The difference between the wholesale and retail price is the dealer's profit.
Historian:	Helena Rubenstein sold her cosmetics in department stores. As a beauty expert, she expanded her business, distributing 160 different products to 3000 retails stores.
Narrator One:	I'd like to invent and develop a product that is sold all over the world.
Rubenstein:	You must work very hard. You must be determined to succeed.
Narrator Two:	Is that all it takes - hard work and determination?
Rubenstein:	No, no. Those are only part of a success story. A successful business needs three things: 1) marketable product, 2) capital or money to get the business started, and 3) "leg-work" or a sales force to sell the product.

Historian:	Helena Rubenstein had marketable products, money to start and run the business, and a successful sales force around the world. She worked tirelessly. She was at her office just two days before she died at the age of ninety-four.
Chorus:	Make me beautiful; make me look great. No trial-and-error approach; nothing to translate.
Historian:	The use of pleasant smelling perfumes and cosmetics has been going on since history has been recorded.
Narrator One:	The next person we'll discuss is D.H. McConnell, who started Avon products in 1886. Welcome to our Readers' Theater play, Mr. McConnell.
McConnell:	Thank you. I'm always happy to talk about my products and company.
Narrator Two:	How did you get started?
McConnell:	In 1886, I was selling door-to-door.
Narrator One:	Did people buy a lot of Avon products in 1886?
McConnell:	When I first got started selling door-to-door, I wasn't selling beauty products. I was selling books.
Narrator Two:	If you were selling books, how did you start the Avon line of beauty products?
McConnell:	Many housewives were not interested in books. I had to think of some way to get their attention and to get them to buy something.
Narrator One:	What did you do?
McConnell:	I made up a small vial of perfume to give to the housewife. A free gift gets people's attention.
Narrator Two:	Did it work? Did the housewives buy books after they got the free perfume?

McConnell:	Not enough to make a living. But I did learn a lesson in this experiment. I discovered that the women wanted the perfume more than the books. Perfume would sell.
Historian:	McConnell's experiment is called "market research." Through his market research he learned that perfume would sell door-to-door.
McConnell:	I quickly abandoned the books and organized the California Perfume Company. I manufactured and sold the perfume door-to-door.
Narrator One:	Did you have enough money to buy a building, perfume-making equipment, and hire people to manufacture and sell the perfume?
McConnell:	My business started as did many successful businesses: in our home. The company started in a room about the size of a kitchen pantry. There were two people: myself and my wife.
Historian:	Many successful businesses started that way. Many more start every year.
McConnell:	During those first years, I filled the positions of bookkeeper, cashier, correspondent, shipping clerk, office boy and manufacturing chemist.
Narrator Two:	But your company is a big successful company.
McConnell:	By 1897, the company had moved to New York. More employees were hired. We sold 18 different perfume fragrances.
Historian:	They also sold baking power, olive oil, flavoring extracts, toothpaste, hair tonic, talcum powder, face powder, and rouge.
McConnell:	The possibilities grew every day.
Narrator One:	Was your company called Avon?

McConnell:	No. The name wasn't given until 1936. In 1936, the company was celebrating its 50th anniversary. I changed the name to Avon.
Narrator Two:	Why Avon?
McConnell:	I personally picked the name because of Shakespeare. Shakespeare was born in Stratford-on-Avon. I had a great love for Shakespeare and my company honors him through its name.
Historian:	To this day, Avon representatives serve almost every community through direct sales to homes.
Narrator One:	Thanks for sharing this information with us, Mr. McConnell.
McConnell:	It has been my pleasure to be here.
Chorus:	Make me beautiful; make me look great. No trial-and-error approach; nothing to translate.
Narrator Two:	Our third guest is Madame C.J. Walker.
Walker:	Thank you for inviting me. My story is a success story in cosmetics and for my race - the black people.
Historian:	Madame Walker was born Sarah Breedlow to former slaves in Louisiana in 1867. She was orphaned at five. At fourteen, she married a man by name of McWilliams.
Walker:	Six years later, he died, leaving me alone to raise a daughter A'Lelia.
Narrator One:	What did you do?
Walker:	I did what any responsible person would do: I figured out a way to take care of my daughter and myself.
Narrator Two:	What did you do?

Walker:	I moved to St. Louis, Missouri. I worked as a washerwoman. That's when my hair began to fall out.
Narrator One:	Your hair fell out? Why?
Walker:	I didn't know <u>why</u> it was falling out. I just knew it <u>was</u> falling out?
Narrator Two:	What did you do?
Historian:	She combined ingredients. The mixture worked.
Walker:	My hair was growing in faster than it was falling out. My friends tried it. It worked for them also.
Historian:	When entrepreneurs see a problem, they find a way to solve it. Then they market that solution. And that's what Sarah did.
Narrator One:	And that's when you became Madame Walker?
Walker:	Not right away. First I had to become Sarah Walker. That happened when I married Charles Walker, a newspaperman in Denver, Colorado.
Narrator Two:	Did he help you with the company?
Walker:	Yes. We advertised in his newspapers. Our advertising was directed towards black women. My people had come from slavery.
Historian:	Slavery keeps your body in one place. But slavery also has the message that you aren't important.
Walker:	My message to black women was that they were free. They <u>were</u> important and they <u>were</u> beautiful.
Historian:	Madame Walker traveled widely and demonstrated her products. She gave more than beauty products. She gave to black women a message that they had dignity.

Walker: Loveliness comes from within the person
- not from the color of the skin. We black
women are beautiful. We should be proud of
who we are and our appearance.

Historian: The Walkers organized "Walker Clubs"
for women. These clubs provided cash
prizes for outstanding community service.

Walker: I also directed fund raising campaigns to establish
Mary McLeod Bethune's school in Daytona.
We also raised funds to pay off the mortgage
on Frederick Douglass's home.

Historian: Madame C.J. Walker became a millionaire. She used
her talents and her money for good causes.

Walker: Be proud of who you are. Let your appearance
give that message of pride.

Narrator: Thank you, Madame Walker. Your message is
one we need to hear.

Chorus: Make me beautiful; make me look great.
No trial-and-error approach; nothing to translate.

Narrator One: Our next guest is Mr. Max Factor.

Historian: Max Factor was a Russian cosmetician who amassed
a great personal fortune applying his artful preparations
to the faces of Hollywood's earliest stars.

Factor: I was born to a poor family. My career in
cosmetics began at age of thirteen. I was thirteen
when I dropped out of a synagogue school to become
a make-up boy with a traveling opera troupe.

Historian: During this apprenticeship, he learned how to
mix powders, shadows and rouges. He also
learned wigmaking.

Factor:	I liked this work. It wasn't traditional men's work but I liked it. And I was good at it. I became the make-up man with the prestigious Russian Royal Ballet.
Historian:	But Max Factor wanted more freedom than czarist Russian could afford.
Factor:	In 1904, at age 27, my wife and I and our three children immigrated to the United States. I set up a wig and makeup concession stand at the St. Louis World's Fair.
Narrator One:	Did people like what you were demonstrating?
Factor:	Very much so. After the Fair, we moved to California where I put in long hours in a one-man shop.
Narrator Two:	What did you sell in the shop?
Factor:	I sold and manufactured beauty products. Our sons, Davis and Max, Jr. helped.
Historian:	The young motion picture industry shifted from New York to California. This was his chance. Max Factor saw his chance and took it.
Narrator One:	What chance was that?
Factor:	The motion picture industry required makeup for close-up shots. The harsh lights needed for shooting film made colors less than true.
Narrator Two:	How did you figure out what was needed?
Factor:	I met with film directors, actors and actresses. I listened to them. Ideas were tested. Most of them worked. My reputation grew - rapidly.
Historian:	Actresses liked the makeup so well that they began to wear it outside the film studios.
Narrator One:	I can understand that. People want to be beautiful all the time.

Factor:	My make-up expertise was associated with beautiful Hollywood actresses in America. By 1927, the products were selling nationally.
Historian:	When Max Factor died of a liver and kidney ailment in 1938, management of the company passed on to sons. The family-run business was America's third largest cosmetics firm in 1973. It was later sold for $480 million dollars.
Chorus:	Make me beautiful; make me look great. No trial-and-error approach; nothing to translate.
Narrator One:	Our last guest is Mary Kay Ash.
Narrator Two:	Is that the "pink Cadillac lady"?
Ash:	Yes, I am the pink Cadillac lady. The pink Cadillac, and the diamond rings, and the luxury vacations are all prizes my sales representatives can earn through their efforts to help people look and feel beautiful.
Historian:	Mary Kay Cosmetics was founded in 1963 by Mary Kay Ash, a retired woman from Hot Wells, Texas.
Ash:	My company offers skin-case products through a sales force recruited from women who want to make a living or supplementary income by marketing these products.
Narrator One:	Did you always want to be in the cosmetics business?
Ash:	I was a straight-A student in high school. I wanted to be a doctor. My family could not afford school for me to become a doctor.
Narrator Two:	So, what did you do?
Ash:	I got married. Divorce followed in eleven years. I supported my family by selling cleaning products through in-home demonstrations.

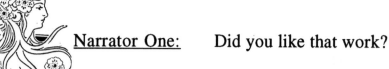

Narrator One:	Did you like that work?
Ash:	It kept a roof over our heads and bread on our table. I didn't stay with that company.
Historian:	She left the company but had learned the method and value of in-home demonstrations and sales.
Ash:	I opened my first retail cosmetic shop on Friday, September 13, 1963. My son soon joined me. We designed a marketing plan that was successful and is still successful today.
Narrator Two:	Can I buy Mary Kay Cosmetics in stores?
Ash:	No. Our method is in-home demonstrations. The motivation for our representatives is profit - profit and prize awards.
Narrator One:	Why are Mary Kay products successful?
Ash:	The answer is simple: People continue to buy because the products, and the sales force, are good.
Historian:	And the appeal of the products is the universal appeal for the human being to appear lovely to oneself and to others.
Chorus:	Make me beautiful; make me look great. No trial-and-error approach; nothing to translate.
Narrator One:	Thank you, Helena Rubenstein, Madame Walker, D. H. McConnell, and Mary Kay Ash.
Narrator Two:	Our Readers' Theater is ended.

The End

John Deere

Cast

> *Farmer One*
> *Farmer Two*
> *John Deere*
> *Sarah Deere, John's mother*
> *William Deere, John's father*
> *Demarius Lamb, John's wife*
> *Narrator*

Modifications you may wish to make:
> *Add local information about John Deere products, dealers*
> *or the use of John Deere products in your geographic area.*

John Deere® is a registered trademark.

Narrator:	Many of us recognize the green and yellow colors that identify the machine as a John Deere implement. It is the inventiveness and creativity of John Deere that is the subject of today's Readers' Theater play.
Sarah Deere:	I am John's mother, Sarah Deere. We lived in the beautiful state of Vermont. We were a happy family.
William Deere:	I am John's father, William Deere. My profession was that of tailor. I made clothes for people. Our shop was in the front of our house.
John Deere:	My name is John Deere. When I was little, I liked to watch the local blacksmith forge and repair metals. The blacksmith worked on horse-shoes, chains, pots and pans.
Farmer One:	I am a farmer. When our farm crops were good, we could buy things. It was a good feeling to be able to order clothes, buy and repair farm equipment, and pay our bills.
Farmer Two:	I also am a farmer. When the farm crops were not good, we could not buy new things. Our bills could not be paid.

Narrator:	Crops were not always good in Vermont. When crops were not good, business was poor. Farmers had little or no money.
Sarah Deere:	When we were short of money, I sewed and mended people's clothes. That brought in a little extra money.
William Deere:	Sarah, I have good news. This letter says I have inherited some money from a relative in England.
Sarah Deere:	This is a blessing. How soon will the money come?
William Deere:	I don't know. I must go to England to get it.
Sarah Deere:	Oh, William. The trip will be dangerous. We will miss you very much.
William Deere:	And I shall miss you and the children. I will be back as soon as possible.
Sarah Deere:	The trip across the Atlantic is always a dangerous trip. It is particularly dangerous now.
Narrator:	William Deere left for England during the time of the French and Indian War. Ships were often sunk. Letters sent were often never received.
Sarah Deere:	William. William. What has happened to you?
Narrator:	William Deere never returned. No one knows what happened to him. He could have died at sea. And the records of his death could have been lost.
Farmer One:	Mrs. Deere, it appears William is not returning. I am sorry for you and your children. Is there anything I can do to help you?
Farmer Two:	We will help you in any way we can. We will help to raise your children.

Sarah Deere:	Thank you. The children and I appreciate your understanding. The children and I will stay together as a family. We will make it.
John Deere:	I'll get a job. That will help the family.
Narrator:	John's first job was grinding bark and oak leaves to create tannin. Tannin is a substance that preserves animal hides. After the hides are preserved, they can be made into leather. Tannin also gives leather a nice tan color.
John Deere:	I am finished with grammar school. I don't need any more schooling.
Sarah Deere:	I want you to go to school a few more years.
John Deere:	Thank you, mother. But I don't want more schooling. I want to work with my hands. I have been watching the blacksmith. I would like to be a blacksmith and work with metals.
Narrator:	John got the opportunity to be an apprentice to Captain Lawrence - the blacksmith. John was delighted. Captain Lawrence had a fine reputation for making and repairing metals.
Sarah Deere:	John, your apprenticeship with Captain Lawrence is now complete. You must move on to the next step of journeyman.
John Deere:	I have a choice of two blacksmiths with whom to study. One specializes in carriage-making. The other specializes in ironwork.
Sarah Deere:	Which will you choose?
John Deere:	I don't want to choose. I want to work with both. There are many skills I could learn from each.
Sarah Deere:	Is that possible?

John Deere:	I will talk to both and see what can be arranged.
Narrator:	And an arrangement was made. John worked with both. It was during this time that he met Demarius Lamb - a young woman from a town in the Green Mountains.
John Deere:	Mother, I'd like you to meet Miss Demarius Lamb. She is a friend.
Sarah Deere:	How do you do, Miss Lamb. I am pleased to meet you.
Demarius:	Thank you, Mrs. Deere. I am pleased to meet you also.
Sarah Deere:	John has told me that you and he are friends. I am happy to meet my childrens' friends.
John Deere:	Demarius and I are more than friends. We are considering marriage.
Narrator:	John Deere and Demarius Lamb were married in 1827. Sarah Deere did not live long enough to share this happy day.
John Deere:	I will start my own blacksmith business. We will soon have a good business.
Demarius:	We will be a happy husband and wife. Our business will be successful.
Narrator:	The Deere's did go into business - twice. And twice fire destroyed their business. The cause of the first fire is unknown. The second fire was started by lightning.
John Deere:	I have no cash to start a third business. I will work for another until I have enough cash to start another business.

Farmer One:	Mr. Deere, I cannot pay my bill with money. But I do have some chickens. Will you accept that as payment?
John Deere:	Yes. These are hard times for all of us.
Farmer Two:	Mr. Deere, I have no money to pay you to fix my plow. I do have vegetables and fruits. Will you accept vegetables and fruits?
John Deere:	Yes. Thank you. Your vegetables and fruits are the finest. We will work together during these hard times.
Demarius:	John, do not feel discouraged. All of the farmers are in hard times. When farmers are having hard times, the merchants who serve them have hard times. We will make it. As long as we receive meat, fruit and vegetables, we will survive.
John Deere:	I knew you were just the right woman to have as a wife. Thank you.
Demarius:	As long as we are together, and we have enough food, all will be well.
John Deere:	I have another plan. I think I should move to another part of the country.
Demarius:	What will you do? Will we go together?
John Deere:	I'll go ahead and make sure there is a good job and place for us.
Demarius:	Send for me as soon as you can.
Narrator:	This major change was made in 1836. John Deere left New England and came to Grand Detour, Illinois. In Illinois, he learned that the farmers were not satisfied with the plows they were using.

Farmer One:	John, you are a blacksmith. Make me a plow that will be better than the one I have.
John Deere:	What is the matter with the plow you are using?
Farmer Two:	It gets stuck in this rich gummy prairie ground.
Farmer One:	The soil here sticks to the plow. I spend too much time cleaning the dirt from the plow.
Narrator:	John thought about this. He tried many ways to make a plow that would work in prairie soil. Prairie soil was not like New England soil. Finally, a better plow was developed.
John Deere:	Mr. Farmer, try this plow. I have reshaped it.
Farmer One:	I have tried it. It works better but the dirt still sticks to it. Try another design.
Narrator:	And he did. John Deere designed and re-designed.
John Deere:	Mr. Farmer, try this plow. See how it works.
Farmer Two:	This is it, Mr. Deere! You did it! This highly-polished, curved and pointed plow is just the ticket for prairie soil.
Narrator:	John was in business. In 1838, Demarius and the children joined him in Illinois.
Demarius:	I always knew John would be a big success.
Farmer One:	And she was right. Whenever we had a problem John would study the problem. Then, through trial and error, he would discover a solution.
Farmer Two:	We could count on John Deere to supply our needs.
Narrator:	By 1842 Deere was selling 100 plows a year.

<u>Farmer One:</u>	By 1843, at age 39, John became an entrepreneur and founded the plow company.
<u>Farmer Two:</u>	By 1857, he was producing 10,000 plows a year.
<u>Narrator:</u>	He died May 17, 1886, at the age of 82. He died in his sleep.
<u>Farmer One:</u>	During his life, John Deere stood for quality farm implements.
<u>Narrator:</u>	To this day, the green and yellow colors of John Deere implements stand for reliable, innovative equipment. You'll see them in stores, on lawns, and in fields. Look for them.

The End

Eyes Products

Cast
> *Narrator*
> *Otis Hall*
> *Doctor One*
> *Doctor Two*
> *Historian*

Modifications you may wish to make:
> *Invite a local ophthalmologist, oculist or optometrist as a guest speaker.*
> *Ask a drug, department, or prescription lenses store, to display a variety of glasses.*

Brand names and/or registered trademarks referenced in this play include Murine.

Narrator: The eye is an extremely sensitive part of the body. It is through the eyes that we learn many things. We communicate with our eyes.

Doctor One: But the eyes, like any other part of the body, can become irritated and impaired.

Doctor Two: When the eyes aren't working correctly, the quality of life is lowered. We cannot see well. We cannot enjoy reading or looking at people and things.

Historian: Eye drops or lotions to soothe and heal eyes have been used for over 5000 years - dating back to the days of China's ancient wisdom.

Doctor One: The Chinese used an eye drop made from the mahuang plant. An ingredient from that plant is ephedrine hydrochloride.

Doctor Two: This ingredient is still used to treat eye irritations, especially allergic reactions.

Historian: In the mid-1800s, Hermann von Helmholtz published a book, HANDBOOK OF PHYSIOLOGICAL OPTICS. He invented the ophthalmoscope for examining the eye's interior. He also invented the ophthalmometer, for measuring the eye's ability to see at varying distances.

Doctor One: Doctors learned that the only solution that was completely
safe for eyes was boiled and cooled sterile water. It is an
ingredient in many eye drops or solutions.

Doctor Two: Sometimes a bit of boric acid is added because
boric acid is a mild antibacterial agent.

Narrator: A gentleman by the name of Mr. Otis Hall played
a part in keeping our eyes healthy and feeling good.

Otis Hall: I learned about a special eye lotion when my eye was hurt.
A horse had swished its tail into my eye. I went to see two
brothers, the Doctors James and George McFatrich. They
were ophthamologists - doctors who specialized in the eye.

Doctor One: We treated Otis Hall with our special lotion. The eye healed.

Doctor Two: Mr. Hall wanted to market our lotion. He
reasoned that if the lotion was helpful for
him, many other people would want it.

Doctor One: We were reluctant to sell it. We preferred to use it with
our patients - where we could monitor the results.

Doctor Two: But Otis Hall was persistent. He kept telling us that
many people would benefit from our lotion.

Otis Hall: I had to use many persuasion tactics before the McFatrich
doctors agreed to market the eye lotion. Finally, the three
of us formed a company and Murine became the product.

Doctor One: We called it Murine because of the main ingredient in the
lotion. The main ingredient is muriate of berberine.

Doctor Two: We took the first three letters of "muriate" and the last
four letters of "Berberine " and created the word Murine.
That's what we called our product.

Narrator: Murine eye lotion is an easily-bought over-the-counter
product. It has been marketed since the late 1890s.

Narrator: Many people need glasses because many eyes are
not perfect. Corrective lens are needed.

Historian: Eye glasses to correct imperfect eye sight were probably invented in Italy in the 13th century. Evidence points to two glass blowers, Alessandro Spina and Salvino Armato.

Doctor One: The first glasses were convex, which aided only far-sighted individuals. By 1326, eye glasses were available to scholars, nobility, and clergy.

Doctor Two: Early eye glasses were hard to keep on because the loop over the ears did not develop until the 18th century.

Historian: With the printing press improvements of the 15th century, and more books available for the general public, the need for glasses increased.

Doctor One: Glasses steadily improved. In the 1760s, Benjamin Franklin experimented with bifocal glasses.

Doctor Two: Bifocals did not come into common use until the 1820s.

Historian: Today, many people prefer contact lens to regular eye glasses. The first person to propose contact lens was Leonardo da Vinci in the 16th century.

Doctor One: Da Vinci's eye-sight correction method was this: place the eye against a short, water-filled tube - sealed at the end of a flat lens. The water comes in contact with the eyeball. The light rays are refracted through the water. This is similar to the way a curved lens refracts light.

Doctor Two: Da Vinci's use of water as the best surface to touch the eye is incorporated into the high water content of today's soft contact lens.

Historian: The first practical contact lenses were developed in 1877 by Swiss physician Dr. A.E. Fisk. These were hard lenses - thick, uncomfortable, unsightly, and heavy.

Narrator: But these first contact lens proved such lens were possible. The product could be improved.

Doctor One: Today, many people wear contact lens. They are of many types and colors, including the yellow contact lens used by Commander Data of "Star Trek".

Doctor Two: Today's contact lens are lightweight, attractive, and highly effective for many people.

Narrator: Sunglasses are another improvement for the eyes. Many people wear them. They wear them to protect eyes from glare. Sunglasses are also part of a fashion statement.

Historian: The first sunglasses were smoke-tinted glasses used in China before 1430. Their original purpose was to serve judges. Judges wore darkened glasses to conceal emotions and reactions which are readily seen in human eyes.

Doctor One: In the 1930s, the United States military wanted glasses to protect pilots from high-altitude glare. As usual, when there is a need, somebody will fill that need. Suitable glasses were developed.

Doctor Two: The sunglasses protected the eyes from glare and foreign objects. The general public became interested. Soon sunglasses were a common item.

Historian: Sunglasses, as part of a fashion statement, were a later development. Companies created special designs. In the 1990's, the brand name was important - more important than the service the glasses provided.

Doctor One: Take care of your eyes. They are sensitive.

Doctor Two: Shield them from foreign objects and excessive glare.

Historian: What will be the next step in the history of eye care?

Doctor One: That is hard to say.

Doctor Two: One thing is certain: new ideas come from new wants and needs.

Narrator: We'll have to wait to see what the new step will be.   *The End.*

Game Developers

Cast
Milton Bradley
Game Player One
Game Player Two
Historian
George Parker

Modification you may wish to make:
Display information about games.

Brand names and/or registered trademarks referenced in this play include:
Monopoly, Clue, Banking.

Historian: The entrepreneurs featured today are inventors and entrepreneurs of games.

Player One: Some people admire military generals. I admire people who can design a game that amuses and holds my interest.

Player Two: Games give value to leisure time. I like games of skill and luck - but mostly skill.

Historian: Our first game entrepreneur is Milton Bradley. Welcome, Mr. Bradley.

Bradley: Thank you. I am happy to be here.

Historian: Mr. Bradley, how did you get started manufacturing games?

Bradley: Abraham Lincoln made me do it.

Player One: Abraham Lincoln? How could he make you market games?

Bradley: He didn't actually <u>make</u> me do it. I started to invent and manufacture games because Abraham Lincoln grew a beard.

Player Two: Explain, please.

Bradley: During the 1860s, Abraham Lincoln was running for president of the United States. At that time, Lincoln did not have a beard on his face.

Player One: But all pictures I have seen show Lincoln with a beard.

Bradley: Exactly. I was a printer in the 1860s. I had printed many Lincoln pictures which I was selling. These pictures showed Lincoln without a beard.

Player Two: What did you do with the beardless pictures?

Bradley: Not much that meant profit for me. I had to destroy them. I faced near financial ruin.

Historian: The thought of financial ruin often forces entrepreneurs to develop new ideas and plans. And that is what happened with Milton Bradley.

Bradley: A friend of mine had suggested that I invent a game. I could print the game whenever the presses were idle.

Player One: What was your first game?

Bradley: It was called the Checkered Game of Life. The game resembled life because you earned points for "Honor" and "Truth". But you lost points for "Intemperance" and "Ruin".

Historian: Milton Bradley personally sold the game in New York and the New England states. He sold 45,000 copies in the first year.

Bradley: The game was a success. I have always been grateful that Lincoln grew a beard. For it was his beard that challenged me to become an inventor and entrepreneur.

Historian: Thank you, Mr. Bradley for visiting us today.

Bradley: It was my pleasure to be here.

Historian: Our second guest is George Parker. George Parker and his brother, Charles Parker, started the Parker Brothers game company. A third brother, Edward, later joined the company.

Player One: I play Monopoly. That is a Parker Brothers game.

Player Two: I play Clue. That's also a Parker Brothers game.

Parker: Games were always my first love. I was just sixteen when I invented my first board game.

Player One: What was it called?

Player Two: How did you play it?

Parker: It was called Banking. It was a borrowing and lending game. I took a three-week leave-of-absence from high school to market my game.

Player One: Did you sell the game?

Parker: I sold 500 copies of the game. I think they sold because everybody likes to pretend they are bankers. These first 500 copies also sold because I was selling right before Christmas.

Player Two: My mom always buys things when young people are selling them. She says that that is the way she gives encouragement to young entrepreneurs.

Parker: Maybe some people bought for that reason. I just know I sold 500 copies. The excitement of creating and marketing a game stayed with me for life.

Historian: Parker did not immediately start a company. First he had to finish high school. Then, to please his parents, he became a reporter for a newspaper.

Parker: In 1886, a serious respiratory sickness forced me to do less strenuous work. As you probably guessed, I went back to my games.

Historian: His brother Charles joined him and the Parker Brothers game company was formed. It has remained a leading developer and marketer of games for generations - even to our present time.

Player One: I'll probably invent a game some day. My game will be a game of skill.

Player Two: I'll wait for you to invent it and then my company will market it. I'm not good at developing games but I can sell things. People smile and buy things when I sell in my neighborhood.

Historian: Maybe someday one of you in our audience will be the next developer that creates the game. Or you may be the entrepreneur who successfully markets it.

Player One: Inventor, make me a game that combines skill and luck. Make it about finding hidden treasures, or decoding secret messages, or something that takes brains and concentration.

Player Two: Entrepreneur, sell me a game that I can play while I'm waiting for my dad to pick me up from school. It should be about things I like: music, history, and frogs.

Bradley: If you have market research that says people will buy it, we can develop a game on music, history and frogs. If we can sell it, our creative minds will develop it.

Parker: Every topic of interest is the possible subject of a game. Our company will create any game that interests a lot of people. A lot of people have to be interested so that we can sell many copies.

Historian: And that is how games are developed. Will the next best-selling game have your name on it?

Players One & Two: You'll never know unless you try!

Bradley, Parker, Historian: See you in the games store, or the toy section of a department store. Good-bye.

The End

Home Remedies

Cast
>*Child One*
>*Child Two*
>*Parent*
>*Doctor*
>*Historian*
>*Smith Brothers*
>*William Luden*
>*Robert Chesebrough*

Modifications you may wish to make
>*Arrange a display of the products discussed in this play:*
>*Smith Brothers Cough Drops, Vaseline Petroleum Jelly,*
>*Luden Cough Drops. Other products may be added.*

Brand names and/or registered trademarks referenced in this play include:
Smith Brothers and Ludens Cough Drops, Vaseline Petroleum Jelly.

Child One: Our play today is about home remedies. Home remedies are used for minor injuries: when we cut ourselves, get a cough, or develop other conditions that show we are less than 100% fit.

Child Two: I'll introduce you to the readers of this play. Our first reader represents parents or guardians.

Parent: I read lines that tell about parents: a mother or a father, or whoever accepts responsibility for children.

Doctor: I'm the doctor. People come to me when home remedies don't cure the problem. They also come to me when they don't know what the problem is, or if they think something may be serious.

Historian: I'm the historian. It is my task to know the facts of history. I tell you things that you need to know.

Smith Brothers: I am only one reader but I represent my brother and myself. We are the Smith Brothers of Smith Brothers cough drops.

William Luden: I represent myself - William Luden,
          developer and marketer of cough drops.
          I am the competition for the Smith Brothers.

Chesebrough: I'm happy to be here with you today.
          My name is Robert Chesebrough. I am the
          discoverer, inventor, and entrepreneur who
          brought you that wonderful, commonly-used
          product: Vaseline Petroleum Jelly.

Child One: Mr. Smith, how did you and your brother
          develop cough drops?

Smith: Before I answer that, I'd like to tell you why
          you cough. People cough to clear the air passages
          of inhaled foreign matter or bodily secretions.

Child Two: When I have a cough, I use cough drops.
          They make my throat feel better. Then
          I stop coughing.

Smith: The ingredients of the cough drop suppress
          coughs. When the coughing is suppressed,
          the body can relax and feel better.

Historian: The Smith Brothers didn't invent cough drops.
          Cough drops were known to exist in Egypt in
          1000 B.C. The Egyptians did not have sugar
          but they did have honey.

Doctor: Basic ingredients suppress coughs. Different
          flavorings give cough drops different tastes.
          Elm bark, eucalyptus oil, peppermint oil, and
          horehound were a few of the ancient additives.

Doctor: Some coughs are eliminated through the use of cough
          drops. If the cough persists, then people come to me.

Historian: The Smith Brothers' real names were William and
          Andrew. They were native to Quebec, Canada.
          They moved to Poughkeepsie, New York, in 1847.

Smith: We wanted to own and manage a restaurant. Our father, James Smith, was a carpenter by trade but he made good candy. He also had a good head for business.

Historian: It is said that a man gave James the recipe for a mixture that would stop coughing. James promptly made a batch of the mixture in his kitchen.

Smith: We, his sons, sold it. When the first batch was sold, dad made another. It, too, quickly sold. Smith Brothers Cough Drops became a popular item.

Historian: Coughs have been around for as long as mankind has had recorded history. There will always be a market for cough drops.

Child One: I like wild cherry. They taste good. They make my tongue all red.

Child Two: My favorite is honey and lemon. The honey tastes sweet and the lemon stops the cough.

Parent: I buy whatever kind the family likes. I can't stand the sound of coughing. Fortunately, cough drops stop most coughing.

Smith: Other manufacturers tried to imitate the Smith Brothers product and the package. We redesigned the package so that our pictures were on the box. Our pictures made our cough drops look special.

Parent: The Smith brothers' pictures are still on the boxes. That's how I know I have the right kind.

Smith: That was our marketing strategy. Other companies could make their box look like ours. But only our brand would show our pictures.

Child One: I tried Luden's cough drops. They also come in honey and lemon, menthol, and wild cherry.

Luden: I am William Luden. My profession was that of
              candy-maker. I, too, developed and marketed
              cough drops.

Child Two: What was your major contribution to the
              cough drop home remedy department?

Luden: I improved the packaging. Now you might think that
              improved packaging is not a major item. But it is.

Parent: I don't care what the package looks like so long
              as the contents stop the cough.

Luden: Certainly. Certainly. However, I do wish to
              point out that packaging is important. And
              I made a major improvement.

Child One: What did you do?

Luden: I packaged the amber-colored cough drops in boxes
              lined with waxed paper. Wax paper kept the cough
              drops from sticking to the box and tasting like cardboard.

Parent: It also keeps the cough drops fresh.
              Thank you for that improvement.

Child Two: Thanks to the Smith brothers and Mr. Luden for
              telling us about cough drops. But I also get cuts.
              Cough drops don't heal cuts.

Doctor: Many of my patients use Vaseline Petroleum Jelly.
              Vaseline Petroleum Jelly was developed by Robert
              Chesebrough. The story of Robert Chesebrough's
              efforts is interesting. The historian will tell it to you.

Historian: In 1859, Robert Augustus Chesebrough was 22. He
              was a struggling chemist in Brooklyn. News arrived
              of the oil strike in Pennsylvania.

Chesebrough: This was good news for Pennsylvania but
              not good news for me I had selected a career
              refining oil into kerosene. With the discovery
              of oil, the kerosene market would fall to nothing.

Historian: Chesebrough was only 22 with a lifetime ahead of him. If there was no career related to kerosene, then he'd have to apply his knowledge of chemistry to another area.

Chesebrough: I went to the oil fields of Pennsylvania to learn all I could learn about the oil business. I didn't know what I wanted to learn but I knew I had to find another career.

Doctor: There were many accidents in the oil fields. Many accidents were cuts and burns. Chesebrough observed that workers applied "rod-wax" to the cuts and burns.

Historian: This rod-wax was a colorless greasy residue that formed around the pump rods of the oil wells. The workers complained that the rod-wax interfered with the pumping of oil. They also willingly used it to cure cuts and burns.

Chesebrough: I wondered what was in this rod-wax that gave it healing power. Since I had observed its healing power many times, I knew there was something in it that could be used for a medicine.

Doctor: Sometimes we do not know why nor how medicine heals. We just know that it works.

Chesebrough: If I was to develop a new career, I had to know what made the substance heal. I took large quantities of rod-wax back to my chemistry laboratory in Brooklyn.

Child One: What did you do in the lab?

Chesebrough: The long methodical research began. I analyzed samples. I mixes samples with other substances. While all this analysis and mixing was going on, I tested the healing power on cuts and burns.

Child Two: How did you test it? Did people come to you when they got cut or burned? Were you a doctor?

Chesebrough: No, I'm not a doctor. No, they didn't come to me when they were hurt.

Historian: He used himself for tests. He cut, scratched, and burned himself to test the effectiveness of the healing power of each substance he produced.

Child One: He shouldn't do that.

Child Two: I wouldn't do that.

Doctor: Good. And see that you don't. Our bodies are not for experimentation.

Chesebrough: I carried the scars of these tests the rest of my life. At that point in my life, success was the important thing.

Parent: I have used Vaseline Petroleum Jelly for as long as I can remember.

Historian: The story of Chesebrough is not complete. No one would buy the product. He had to design a marketing plan that would work.

Chesebrough: After the product was developed, I raised money to set up a factory to manufacture it. Sales were slow.

Historian: Free samples were sent. Not many orders came in - just requests for more free samples.

Child One: Why buy merchandise if you can get free samples?

Child Two: But sales must have improved. What did you do?

Chesebrough: I set out with horse and buggy. I gave samples to every one I met. I stopped at farm houses and gave samples. Local druggists were then obligated to sell the product since it was the druggist who received requests from local customers.

Doctor: The product caught on. Within a few years, doctors and the general public were buying a jar of Vaseline Petroleum Jelly at the rate of a jar a minute.

Chesebrough:Over the years, Vaseline Petroleum Jelly has been
used for many things. Some common uses are:
remove white rings from mahogany furniture,
polish patent leather, simulate tears on movie sets,
preserve artists' paint brushes. Fisherman use
it for trout bait. Cosmetic manufacturers use it
for the base of beauty creams. Pharmaceutical
companies combine it with other drugs.

Historian: More uses continue to be reported to corporate
headquarters.

---optional---
Readers and audience may add other uses for the product.

Parent: With home remedies, my children and I can treat
many minor discomforts. These remedies give us
quick relief and save money.

Doctor: Many of these remedies work. When you are
buying a home remedy, make sure the product
is approved by the government.

Parent/Child One/Child Two:
Thanks to you, Mr. Smith, Mr. Luden, and Mr. Chesebrough
for making these home remedies possible.

Smith/Luden/Chesebrough: You're welcome.

Doctor/Parent:Take care of yourself.

All: Good-bye.

The End.

Ice Cream - Entrepreneurs

Cast
Narrator
Ice cream Enjoyer One (One)
Ice cream Enjoyer Two (Two)
Ice cream Enjoyer Three (Three)
Ice cream Enjoyer Four (Four)
Ice cream Enjoyer Five (Five)
Ice cream Enjoyer Six (Six)

Modifications you may wish to make:
Add information about local ice cream sources.

Brand names and/or registered trademarks referenced in this play include:
Howard Johnson, Baskin-Robbins, Eskimo Pie.

One: What is your favorite ice cream?

Two: Do you like to eat ice cream just like it is
- or do you want to add something to it
- like hot fudge, caramel or fresh fruit?

Three: Is there ice cream in your freezer - right now?
If you answer yes, is there more than one flavor?

Four: The most popular flavor is strawberry.
Would that be your favorite?

Five: Do you like ice cream in a bowl, frozen on
a stick, squeezed between two cookies - like
an ice cream sandwich?

Six: If you have opinions and answers to these questions,
you are among the millions of people around
the world who like to eat ice cream.

Narrator: Ice cream is enjoyed by people of all ages.
Several entrepreneurs added enjoyment to
our lives by the ice cream they developed.

Narrator: Today, we'll talk about four people who contributed to the ice cream industry. These four people are: Howard Johnson, Burton Baskin, Irvine Robbins, and Christian Nelson.

One: Two of these four joined forces to form **Baskin-Robbins.**

Two: Irvine Robbins learned about ice cream while working at his father's dairy business. He experimented with unusual flavor combinations.

One: Burton Baskin learned about ice cream while working in the navy. He obtained an ice cream freezer from an aircraft carrier supply source. Baskin made creamy frozen ice cream treats by adding local tropical fruits.

Two: Baskin and Robbins were brothers-in-law. That means their wives were sisters. They formed a business partnership in 1947.

One: The partnership was a good one. They got along very well because they agreed that they should sell nothing but ice cream.

Two: Their first goal was to make $75 a week. When they reached that goal - which they quickly did - they set new sales' goals.

One: By the second year they had 8 southern California stores. They wanted to expand but they didn't have enough money to buy stores and hire people to run them.

Two: Baskin & Robbins did what many others do: they developed and sold franchises for their product.

Narrator: A franchise is a business agreement that works well for many products.

Five: How does a franchise work?

Narrator: A dealer buys a franchise for the product - in this case Baskin-Robbins ice cream. Baskin-Robbins supplies the ice cream, merchandising aids, and major advertising campaigns.

Four: If Baskin-Robbins does all that, how do they make any money?

Narrator: The buyer buys the franchise, purchases or rents a building, hires employees, and is in charge of everyday details of a business.

Three: I still don't understand how Baskin-Robbins makes money from a franchise.

Narrator: Money - often a large sum - is paid for the franchise. The franchise owner also buys the ice cream from Baskin-Robbins. In a good franchise, both businesses make money. They are mutually dependent.

One: Baskin-Robbins ice cream concentrates on 31 flavors - one for each day of the month. These flavors rotate.

Two: They also give unusual names to their flavors - like ChaChaCha - a combination of cherry chocolate chip. Fudge brownie ice cream was first developed by them.

One: Some flavors were tested but never marketed - like the "ketchup" ice cream.

Two: Some flavors were marketed but withdrawn from the market - such as Goody Goody Gumdrop. The gumdrop ice cream was withdrawn because the gum drops became hard as rocks when frozen into ice cream.

One: By 1967, there were 500 Baskin-Robbins stores.

Two: By 1978, more than 2000 stores were operating in the United States, Canada, Japan and Europe.

Narrator: Another entrepreneur who made his fortune and mark in the world through ice cream was Howard Johnson.

Three: Howard Johnson started his work in Massachusetts. The "secret recipe" for ice cream was purchased from an elderly German pushcart vendor.

Four: Johnson sold this ice cream in his drug store. Pushcart vendors also sold the ice cream on the beach, near theaters and stores.

Narrator: Pushcart vendors sell wherever there are people who'd be interested in the products they are selling.

Three: Howard Johnson, like Baskin Robbins, also sold his ice cream through franchises.

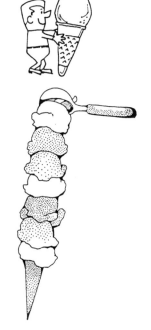

Four: Johnson was like Baskin and Robbins in that he also insisted on high standards at all times.

Three: Howard Johnson specialized in 28 flavors. He himself kept ten flavors in his home freezer.

Four: Howard Johnson was an unorthodox executive who - even when his company went over the $100 million dollars a year level - did not have a secretary or a regular office.

Three: True to his own company and taste, Johnson ate at least one ice cream cone a day.

Four: For breakfast, he often had a bowl of cereal topped with a scoop of banana ice cream.

Narrator: Sounds like a good way to live. Our play now moves on to another entrepreneur in the ice cream field. That is Christian Nelson - the designer and marketer of ice cream on a stick - the Eskimo Pie.

Five: Christian Nelson was a Danish immigrant and school teacher. He died on March 8, 1992. He was 98 years old.

Six: In his lifetime, he did many things. But he is known to the world for only one of those things: frozen ice cream on a stick, with chocolate on the outside.

Five: Nelson owned and operated an ice cream parlor in Onawa, Iowa. One day an 8-year-old boy with one nickel couldn't decide if he should spend his nickel for a candy bar or for a scoop of ice cream.

Six: Entrepreneurs have a way of responding to problems - like the boy's indecision. Something in their brain starts to stir, to move around, to rearrange previous knowledge and ideas.

Five: And so it was with Nelson when the boy could not decide which would taste better - the scoop of ice cream or the candy bar.

Six: Nelson experimented with chocolate and with ice cream. He added coconut oil to heated chocolate. With that blend, the chocolate would stick to the ice cream.

Five: His first attempts to market it did not succeed. First attempts often don't succeed.

Six: But entrepreneurs are not easily discouraged. They back off for awhile. They think. And the successful ones will try again.

Five: The original name for the Eskimo Pie was "I-Scream Bar." He later joined with candy-maker Russell Stover to patent and market Eskimo Pies.

Six: His ice cream invention and treat was a success in the 1920's. It is still a success today.

Narrator: And what will be the ice cream sensation of tomorrow?

One: We don't know because we, the readers of this play, and you - the audience here today, are still thinking about it.

Two: I'd like to try "dill-chip" ice cream.

Three: What would be in that?

Two: Dill pickles and potato chips.

Four: I'd like ice cream that could be packed into lunch boxes.

Five: That's impossible because the ice cream would melt.

Four: It's not impossible. It just hasn't been
           done - yet. I'm working on it.

Six: I want an ice cream that is made of all natural
           products, is healthy, tastes good, is inexpensive,
           and comes in fifteen flavors.

Five: Why fifteen flavors?

Six: Because my birthday is the 15th. And it was on my
           15th birthday, on the 15th day of May, that I made a
           list of 15 flavors I'm going to have for my new ice cream.

Five: What are the 15 flavors?

Four: What will be in your ice cream?

Three: How will you manufacture it to keep the price down?

Two: How soon will it be available?

Six: All those answers are stored in my brain and my
           lab notes. Entrepreneurs - if they are smart - don't
           reveal secrets before patents or copyrights are
           in the process. I learned that from a book.

Three: Hurry up. Your public is waiting!

Narrator: *(motions to audience)* And your public is waiting
           - for your ideas! And this play is ended.

The End

Inventions and Entrepreneurs

Cast

Chorus
Narrator One
Narrator Two
Challenger (always wanting better things)
Responder (to the one who challenges)
Inventor One
Inventor Two

Modifications you may wish to make:
Add information about inventions and inventors from your geographic area.
Reassign the inventors and narrators parts for more readers to
take part in the play.

Challenger:	Make my life easier, happier, better and stronger. Like: shoes that grow larger when my feet get longer.
Responder:	That's a great idea. Invent it yourself. Then be an entrepreneur and market it.
Chorus:	Inventions help the world improve and grow. Some inventions are useful; some are just so-so.
Narrator One:	There are inventions that have played major roles in world civilizations.
Inventor One:	Inventions that moved civilization forward include the wheel, and the needle.
Inventor Two:	Other inventions were the abacus for counting, the bow and arrow for hunting, coins and money for trading, and irrigation systems for agriculture.
Narrator Two:	Who invented the wheel, needle, abacus, money, and irrigation systems?
Inventor One:	History records no inventors.
Inventor Two:	We can only be grateful for the inventions.

Narrator One:	Are there other inventions that play a major part in our lives for which no inventor can be credited?
Inventor One:	Yes. We don't know who invented the potter's wheel, the pulley, the rope, the shovel, and the sled.
Inventor Two:	We do know that a waterwheel with gears was developed by the Romans by 50 B.C. The principle of the waterwheel to generate power is still used today.
Chorus:	Inventions help the world improve and grow. Some are useful; some are just so-so.
Challenger:	Stop talking about all those common ordinary things. Make me inventions that give my life wings.
Responder:	Like what?
Challenger:	Like snow melting sticks and self-repairing bricks.
Responder:	Those are great ideas. Invent them yourself. Then be an entrepreneur and market them.
Narrator Two:	Some inventions made our lives healthier.
Inventor Two:	Inventions that made our lives healthier include: polio vaccine - developed during the years 1952-1955, the stethescope developed in 1816, and food canning processes refined in the years 1795-1809.
Narrator One:	Some inventions make our lives happier and safer.
Inventor One:	These inventions include the telephone in 1876, the radio in 1895, and the zipper in 1893.
Challenger:	Clothes. Clothes mean a lot to me. Make me clothes that make me look great!
Responder:	That can never be.

Inventor One:	Inventions are made by people who refuse to accept that something can never be.

Challenger:	You mean that maybe, someday, an inventor will invent clothes that make me look great?

Inventor One:	It could be. Inventions, and the entrepreneurs who market the inventions, are people who believe all things are possible.

Chorus:	Inventions help the world improve and grow. Some are useful; some are just so-so.

Narrator One:	Some inventions improved farming. With improved farming equipment, it was easier to provide sufficient food for people and animals.

Narrator Two:	Some of these inventors and their inventions are: James Small of Scotland, who invented the cast iron plow in 1784.

Inventor One:	Eli Whitney of United States invented the cotton gin in 1793. The cotton gin picked the seed from the cotton.

Inventor Two:	Cyrus McCormick of the United States invented the reaper in the 1833. Grain could be harvested quicker and with less loss.

Narrator One:	Some inventions improved communications. It is communication systems that provide information.

Narrator Two:	The inventions, and the entrepreneurs who marketed them, have made it possible for families and countries to communicate with each other.

Inventor One:	1836. Telegraph - Samuel Morse. 1861. Motion picture projector - Coleman Sellers. 1876. Telephone - Alexander Graham Bell.

Inventor Two:	1877. Phonograph - Thomas Alva Edison. 1884. Fountain pen - Lewis E. Waterman. 1895 Wireless telegraphy - Marconi.

Chorus:	Inventions help the world improve and grow. Some are useful; some are just so-so.
Narrator One:	Necessity is the mother of invention.
Challenger:	What exactly does that mean?
Narrator One:	That means that we wish there was something - a machine or a device - that would make our work easier, quicker or more enjoyable.
Responder:	You mean - like calculators, computers and safe, efficient cars?
Narrator One:	Yes. And because someone wants it, inventors will work to make it happen.
Narrator Two:	Some inventions are also machines or devices that add to our enjoyment, delight and entertainment.
Challenger:	Like skates, video games, and bubble gum?
Narrator Two:	Yes.
Chorus:	Inventions help the world improve and grow. Some are useful; some are just so-so.
Narrator One:	Some inventors invented many things.
Narrator Two:	Galileo and Ben Franklin were such inventors.
Inventor One:	Galileo was an Italian scientist who lived from 1564-1642. He invented many things - including the compound microscope and the thermometer.
Inventor Two:	Benjamin Franklin invented the bifocal lens and the lightning rod.

Narrator One: Some inventors and their inventions made travel faster, safer, and more enjoyable. Some of these are:

Inventor One: Rocket - Sir William Congreve, 1804.

Inventor Two: Steamboat - Robert Fulton, 1807.

Inventor One: Steam locomotive - George Stephenson, 1814.

Inventor Two: Vulcanized rubber - Charles Goodyear, 1844.

Inventor One: Pullman sleeping car - George M. Pullman, 1864.

Inventor Two: Bicycle - Pierre Lallement, 1865.

Inventor One: Motor car - F.A. J. Loffler, 1884.

Challenger: I thought Henry Ford invented the motor car.

Responder: No. Henry Ford invented the assembly-line method for producing cars.

Challenger: Is that so great?

Responder: Yes. Assembly-line production insured consistency of product and less costly production. The reduced cost made it possible for more people to own a car.

Narrator One: Inventions improve our lives.

Narrator Two: Inventions, and the entrepreneurs who market them, make our lives easier, happier, healthier and safer.

Chorus: Thank you, inventors. Thank you, entrepreneurs.

The End

Inventions that Delight Us

Cast

Salesperson One
Salesperson Two
Buyer One
Buyer Two
Inventor - represents many inventors
Entrepreneur - represents many entrepreneurs

Modifications you may wish to make;
Add other information you may wish to add.

Brand names and/or registered trademarks referenced in this play include:
Atari, Birdseye, Levi, Biro, Bic, and Gerber's.

Sales One: Step this way. Buy this product.
It will make your life happy.
It will amuse your children.
It will give you free time.

Buyer One: Salespeople are always promising that their products will
make our lives happier, healthier, freer, and easier.

Buyer Two: They also promise to keep your children entertained - with
"good, clean, wholesome fun" - at reasonable prices.

Sales Two: You folks are skeptical. I don't blame you.
But this time we speak the truth.

Buyer One: All right. All right. We are listening.

Buyer Two: Tell us about these wonderful products, their inventors, and
the companies they started. And how they improved our lives.

Sales One: First will be the Atari video games.

Inventor: In 1972, Noland Bushnel, a 28-year old,
invented the first video game.

Entrepreneur: He formed his own company "Atari."
By 1975, he was producing many games.

Sales Two: Next product: Birdseye frozen foods.

Inventor: Clarence Birdseye lived with Eskimos in Laborador, Canada. There he saw how the Eskimos preserved food by fast freezing it in the cold dry air. When the food was thawed, it tasted good and fresh.

Entrepreneur: He perfected the method so that he could control all factors of the food. The Birdseye frozen food company was his successful venture.

Sales One: Levi jeans.

Inventor: Levi Strauss wanted to find gold in the gold fields of California. He joined the trek of people. He brought along rolls of canvas which he thought he could sell for tents and tops of covered wagons.

Entrepreneur: Instead of selling the canvas for tents, he sewed it to men's trousers to make them stronger. After awhile, he switched from canvas to a heavy cotton. Strauss added special rivets to the corners of pockets to make them stronger. You know them today as jeans.

Sales Two: Rubber bicycle tires.

Inventor: John Dunlop made a rubber tire for bicycles. Before the rubber tire, tires were made of iron. This made a very bumpy ride. Dunlop's tire was a rubber tire with air-filled inner tubes. This tire gave a smoother ride.

Entrepreneur: He patented the invention in 1888. He, himself, didn't start the company to manufacture tires, but he kept shares in the company.

Sales One: Ball point pens.

Inventor: Ladislao Biro invented the ball point pen. He manufactured the new pen and called it a Biro.

Entrepreneur: He did not have enough money to create a bigger factory, so he sold the company to a French firm, Bic. Bic sells over 12 million pens a day.

Sales Two: Baby food.

Inventor: Dan Gerber was the entrepreneur behind Gerber's Baby Food. The need for making strained baby food came from his own experiences with this daughter. He learned, first hand, how much time and mess were involved in preparing strained vegetables for babies.

Entrepreneur: So Gerber thought there should be profit in marketing strained vegetables. The first batches were made and tested. Samples were given to mothers. After the samples were gone, parents willingly paid the price asked.

Sales One: Disposable diapers.

Inventor: Vic Mills was director of Procter & Gambles' development division. He gained first hand experience with diapers while babysitting his grandchild. He learned that diapers were not leak-proof. They also contributed to rash on baby's skin. Traveling with an infant was not always a pleasant experience.

Entrepreneur: He brought this matter up in several product-development meetings. Through trial and error, a disposable diaper was made that satisfied many people. The disposable required less work and kept babies drier. There was less danger of rash. Traveling with a baby could be pleasant.

Sales Two: Step this way. Buy these products. They will make you happy. They will amuse your children. They will give you free time.

Buyer One: Salespeople are always promising that their products will make our lives happier, healthier, freer, and easier.

Buyer Two: And many times they are right.

Inventor: Thus has it been and thus will it continue.

Entrepreneur: And I'll work with you *(motions to audience)* to turn your invention or good idea into a profitable business. Will you be my partner?

Buyers One & Two: We'll be waiting. So long.

The End

Kitchen Time & Energy Savers

Cast

> Child One
> Child Two
> Child Three
> Parent
> Historian One
> Historian Two

Modifications you may wish to make:

> *Invite a kitchen appliance representative from your area*
> *to demonstrate the latest "kitchen time and energy saver."*

Child One:	It's your turn to take the dishes out of the dishwasher.
Child Two:	No it's not. I did it the last time.
Parent:	Stop arguing. It only takes a minute.
Child One:	It may take a minute but it's not my turn to give the minute.
Parent:	Such complaining. It could be like the old days when you had to wash and dry dishes by hand.
Child Three:	Couldn't your family afford a dishwasher?
Child Two:	You didn't have a dishwasher?
Historian One:	Dishwashers weren't invented until the 1880's.
Child One:	Who invented the dishwasher?
Historian Two:	Josephine Cochrane, the wife of an Illinois politician.
Child Two:	I thought the wife of a politician would have servants to do her dishes.
Parent:	She did. But the servants, like you children, often broke dishes. When dishes were broken, she had to order replacements. Replacements cost money. It also took time for replacements to arrive.

Child Three: How did she invent the dishwasher?

Historian One: She measured the dishes. Next wire compartments
                 were fashioned for the plates, saucers and cups.
                 These wire structures were attached to a rotating
                 wheel. A motor turned the wheel.

Child One: Where did the water come from?

Historian Two: Hot soapy water shot up through nozzles at
                 the bottom of the container. It worked.

Child Two: Did she make a fortune on her invention?

Parent: A new idea takes time to interest people.
                 People who entertained a lot where interested.
                 Their servants also broke many dishes.

Historian One: Restaurants also were interested. Restaurants have
                 many dishes to wash and many dishes are broken.
                 Restaurants and hotels were her main customers.

Parent: The first dishwashers were large. In 1914,
                 Mrs. Cochrane's company designed a dishwasher
                 for the a regular home. Regular homes needed
                 a smaller version of the large capacity washer
                 required by a hotel or restaurant.

Historian Two: But the small dishwashers did not sell. One of
                 the reasons they did not sell was because many
                 homes in 1914 did not have electricity or hot water.

Child One: If they had electricity and hot water,
                 I bet they wanted a dishwasher.

Parent: Not really. There was another problem.

Child Two: What was that?
Parent: Many housewives did not mind washing dishes.
                 In fact, some thought it was a pleasant task.

Child Two: They should come here and do our dishes.

Historian One:	Through market research, the company understood why dishwashers for the home were not selling. So they designed an advertising campaign that said dishwashers kept a home healthy.
Child Three:	How can a dish washer keep a home healthy?
Historian Two:	The water used in a dishwasher is hotter than the human hand can stand. The hot water and soap would kill germs.
Child One:	Did that sell home dishwashers?
Historian One:	No. Dishwashers in the home still did not sell very well.
Parent:	The change came in the 1950s. From the 1950s to the present day, people spend less time on routine household tasks. Dishwashers are common items in many households.
Child One:	The dishwasher stores the dirty dishes so that your kitchen looks cleaner.
Parent:	Rough hands and broken fingernails which can accompany washing dishes are eliminated when a machine does the job.
Child Two:	And the hot soapy water does contribute to the sanitary conditions of dishes.
Historian Two:	Dishwashers are here to stay.
Child Three:	I want a dishwasher in my house. I want all the time and energy savers I can get.
Parent:	Be ready to work hard each day to afford them.

Historian One:	The toaster and the can opener are two other kitchen time and energy savers.
Child One:	You mean there was a time when people didn't have a can opener or a toaster?
Child Two:	How did they toast their bread - over a fire?
Child Three:	How did they open a can of refried beans?
Historian One:	Peter Durand, a British merchant, developed the tin can to preserve food. This was in 1810. It did not become popular in the United States until the Civil War in the 1860s.
Historian Two:	The war necessitated canned foods. The first cans for food were heavy and thick-walled. Regular tools, like a hammer and chisel, were used to open them.
Historian One:	When cans became thinner, a device specially made for opening them became important.
Parent:	Inventors are people who respond to a need. A simpler way to open tin cans was the need.
Historian Two:	Ezra J. Warner of Waterbury, Connecticut, patented the first can opener in 1858. It looked like a combination weapon and farm implement but it did open cans. The can opener did not become popular until the Civil War.
Child One:	How could a war make a can opener popular?
Historian One:	It became popular during the Civil War because military people had to rely upon canned goods for food.
Child Two:	If Warner's can opener looked like a weapon, the Civil War soldier could fight with it and open his tin of food.
Child Three:	Good idea. Is that the way it was?
Historian Two:	No.

Parent:	Someone must have invented another can opener because today's openers do not look like a weapon or a farm implement.
Historian One:	The can opener was improved through an invention by William W. Lyman. His device was patented in 1870. Lyman's device had a cutting wheel that moved along the edge of the can.
Child One:	Now we know how the can opener was invented. But you said the toaster was also an invention.
Historian One:	People have been toasting their bread since the days of the Egyptians. The Egyptians toasted or parched their bread to remove moisture. This preserved the bread.
Historian Two:	For thousands of years people had toasted bread over fires. Some of the bread tasted good and some of it -- not so good.
Parent:	Toast tastes good and is easy to make. How was the toaster invented?
Historian One:	The first patent for the pop-up toaster was filed by Charles Strite, of Stillwater, Minnesota, on May 29, 1919.
Historian Two:	The first toasters put on quite a show. The bread would pop up - sometimes quite high. This amused observers.
Child One:	Did it work right? Did it make good toast?
Historian One:	No, not at first. It needed some adjustments.
Child Two:	What kind of adjustments?
Historian Two:	The toasting element needed adjustments. The first piece of toast was often quite pale. The next few pieces came out just right. And toast after that often was burned - but maybe you like it that way!

Historian One:	Restaurants, who served toast in large quantities, definitely wanted a toaster.
Historian Two:	And with an assured market, inventors improved the toaster and entrepreneurs marketed it.
Parent:	In this family, everybody makes their own toast. We each like it a certain way.
Child Three:	I like my toast very dark with peanut butter on it.
Child Two:	I like mine medium dark - whole wheat toast that gives me a nutritious start for the day.
Child Three:	I like my toast any way the toaster gives it. Once I put butter on it, it doesn't make any difference how light or dark it is.
Historian One:	The toaster steadily improved until it would turn out consistently toasted bread - just the way you like it.
Historian Two:	Think about the inventors and entrepreneurs who used their creative talents to develop things we like.
Parent:	I'm glad our home has the time and energy savers we talked about today.
Child One:	I'm glad we have a dishwasher.
Child Two:	Our can opener works just fine.
Child Three:	And our toaster gets a workout every morning.
Historian One:	What will our next time and energy saver be?
Historian Two:	(motions to audience) Will you be the one to invent it?
All:	Good-bye.

The End

Mail Order Entrepreneurs

Cast

> *Shopper One*
> *Shopper Two*
> *Montgomery Ward*
> *James Cash Penney*
> *Richard Sears*
> *Alvah Roebuck*
> *Calendar*

Modifications you may wish to make:
> *Display catalogs from Penney, Sears and Wards.*
> *Display catalogs from other mail-order companies.*

Brand names and/or registered trademarks referenced in this play include:
Montgomery Wards, J.C. Penney, Sears and Roebuck.

Calendar : The time is 1844 - 1913. Aaron Montgomery Ward, the American businessman, pioneered the mail-order business.

One: I live in a small town. Our general store does not have all the merchandise that we need.

Two: I live on the farm. Our roads are muddy. We are often without the things we need.

Ward: I was a traveling salesman in the Middle West. I saw that people in small communities and on farms were not able to get the things they needed.

Calendar: It didn't take Ward long to develop a marketing plan to fill these needs.

Ward: The idea came to me that I could buy merchandise in large quantities from manufacturers for cash. I could sell this merchadise directly to farmers for cash.

Calendar: In 1872, Ward and his partner began a mail-order business.

Ward: My partner, George R. Thorne, and I began our business
         with $2,400 in capital and a one-page catalog. Our office
         was a livery stable loft. We offered dry goods.

One: Now I am seldom without the things I need.
         The items are delivered to me.

Two: It may take awhile for them to come, but now
         everyone can have the things they need.

Calendar: Aaron Montgomery Ward was the pioneer in mail-order
         catalog sales. Two others are now equally famous:
         James C. Penney and the team of Sears and Roebuck.

Penney: I am J. C. Penney. I was born on a farm in the country near
         Hamilton, Missouri, in 1875. My father was a minister.
         There wasn't much money. And there were 12 children.

One: I trust J.C. Penney to give me prompt and reliable service.

Two: I order things from the J.C. Penny catalog. There is
         an 800-telephone number. The products are delivered
         to the store or directly to my home.

One: Shopping at Penney's has been a tradition with our family.

Penney: When I was a child, I worked odd jobs to earn $3.50
         to buy a $1.00 pair of shoes. With the remaining money,
         I bought a pig. I planned to feed the pig and then sell it
         for a profit.

Calendar: Was your plan successful?

Penney: After I spent money to buy the pig, there was no money
         left to buy food for the pig. I had to find a way to feed it.

Calendar: What did you do?

Penney: I made agreements with the neighbors. I'd collect
         their food scraps to feed to the pig. In return for
         the food scraps, I'd clean their garbage pails. This
         plan worked. The pig sold for a profit.

Calendar: Penney's first jobs were in department stores. He started his own business in Kemmerer, a southwestern Wyoming mining town. He called his company the Golden Rule Store. He believed in high principles.

One: I trust some business people and some I do not trust.

Two: Penney built his company on the premise that good ethics and good business could go together.

Penney: I put a price tag on each item. Now customers knew exactly what the price would be. Before I began to mark individual items, the customers had to bargain with the shopkeeper.

One: I don't like to bargain with the shopkeeper. I prefer J.C. Penney's way of marking each items.

Two: I agree. I want to know that all customers are paying the same price for the identical item.

Penney: By 1913, I had 36 stores. That same year, I changed the store name from the Golden Rule store to J.C. Penney. I expanded services to large cities as well as small towns.

Calendar: In 1927, the J.C. Penney company celebrated its 25th anniversary. In that same year, there were 892 stores which sold more than $151 million in sales.

Penney: A company must continuously raise its goals. My goal was a billion dollar sales in a year.

Calendar: The J.C. Penney company met that goal in 1951.

One: It sounds as if Penney had no major setbacks. Is that true?

Two: Most companies had trouble during the Great Depression which started in 1929.

Penney: The Great Depression hit me and my company just
            like it did everyone else. I was worth about $40 million
            in 1929. Like almost every one else, I lost it all.

Calendar: But the entrepreneur keeps going. Penney began to rebuild.
            He traveled to his stores and personally waited on customers.
            He insisted on courtesy and helpfulness at all times.

Penney: When I retired, I established the James C. Penney
            Foundation. The Foundation supports educational,
            religious, scientific projects. My legacy to the world
            is quality merchandise and services.

One: Today's catalog shoppers can shop from Wards, J.C. Penney,
            Sears, and many other companies. We have choices.

Two: Each catalog carries items that meet the needs of someone.

Calendar: The time in 1863. The place is Stewartville, Minnesota.
            Richard Sears was born. He took after his blacksmith father
            who liked to do business in a showy flamboyant style.

Sears: I learned to be a telegrapher and worked for the
            railroad. There were times when I wasn't really busy.
            During my spare time, I sold coal, lumber, and other
            goods which could be shipped by railroad.

Calendar: An entrepreneur has a sense of when some item
            or service will sell. The chance came to Sears in
            1886, when a shipment of watches arrived by rail.
            The local jeweler said he never ordered them.

Sears: I bought each watch for $12 and sold each for $14.
            The $2 profit on each watch was some of the easiest
            money I had earned. So I started the Sears Watch
            Company in a rented office.

Calendar: And again, the large company had a small beginning.
            The first office had a kitchen table and one chair.

Sears: But the watches continued to sell. I thought
I could make more money if I assembled the
watches. So I advertised for a watch maker.

Roebuck: And that's how I, Alvah Roebuck, come into the
picture. I was hired to assemble the watches.

Sears: Mr. Roebuck was exactly what I needed.

Roebuck: We made a great team. Our combined efforts and abilities
enabled our company to grow. We served consumers
through sales made in stores and mail orders.

Sears: Today, the corporate offices are at Sears
Tower in Chicago, Illinois.

Calendar: With the help of the two shoppers, let's compare
some prices from a 1902 Sears and Roebuck
catalog with prices in the early 1990s.

Sears & Roebuck: This should be interesting.

Calendar: Violins.

One: In the 1990s, violin prices ranged from $450 to
$30,000 and up for hand-made European models.

Sears: Our 1902 catalog listed 12 models, ranging
in price from $2.45 to $19.95

Calendar: Wedding rings - bands with no gem stones.

Two: In the 1990s, gold wedding bands, no gems,
ranged in price from $125 to $250. In those
prices, you could choose from about 150 rings.

Roebuck: In 1902, we offered 28 styles ranging in price
from 45 cents to $1.70.

Calendar: Butter churns.

One: The only place to look for butter churns today
        is at antique sales.

Sears: In 1902, we offered 8 models of butter churns.
        Prices ranged from 92 cents - $19.50.

Calendar: Suspenders - those devices placed over
            the shoulders and hooked onto the trousers.

Two: Current prices are $7.50 - $10.00.
        There are two basic models: those that
        button and those that clip onto the trousers.

Roebuck: Suspenders were a great item. We showed 20 models so
            men of all distinctions could be selective. Prices ranged
            from 12 cents to 90 cents - for an embroidered satin pair.

Calendar: Go to your library to see if it has copies of current
            and old catalogs. You will find them very interesting.

Ward: Mail order is a great way to shop.

Penney: You can take your time.

Sears: You don't need a babysitter.

Roebuck: Merchandise is delivered directly to your door.

One & Two: What a great way to shop!

The End

Popcorn

Cast
> *Consumer*
> *Historian*
> *Popcorn*
> *Popcorn Grower*

Modifications you may wish to make
> *Invite local popcorn growers or dealers as guests of honor.*
> *Hold a "popcorn taste test" using 3 or more brands.*

Brand names and/or registered trademarks references in this play include:
Orville Redenbacher Gourmet Popcorn, Snappy Popcorn

Popcorn: I am Popcorn. I am that wonderful seed that pops into fluffiness.

Consumer: I like you. You are easy to prepare - especially the bags that go into the microwave.

Popcorn: I make a major contribution to the world. I promote your health. And I don't cost a lot of money.

Historian: Popcorn has been eaten for at least 5000 years. The process of popping corn was perfected by Native Americans. The Native Americans had three methods for popping corn.

Popcorn: One method required putting an ear of popping corn on a stick and holding the stick over the fire. As the kernels popped free, they were eaten.

Historian: Another method was to toss high-moisture corn kernels directly unto the fire. As the kernels popped and leaped free of the fire, they were eaten.

Popcorn: The third method was a clever method. Sand was placed in a clay pot. The pot with sand was heated. When the sand became hot, the corn was stirred into the sand. The cover was put on the pot and the corn began to pop. As it popped, the corn rose above the sand and was eaten.

Consumer: That's a great idea. My friends and I should try that when we go camping.

Historian: Small home and large store popcorn poppers have been successfully marketed since the 1880's. Today, much popcorn is popped in microwave ovens in specially-designed bags.

Consumer: The ease and speed of making fresh popcorn in the microwave fits my lifestyle.

Grower: I raise popcorn and sell it to you. I really don't care how you pop it. I just want you to buy it.

Consumer: We are eating more and more popcorn each year. It is handy, inexpensive, and good for us.

Grower: Such praise for popcorn is music to my ears.

Popcorn: I am a seed. Why do I pop into a fluffy kernel?

Grower: Corn that will pop has moisture inside. The corn pops when the moisture inside of it turns to steam. The hot steam causes the corn kernel to explode. An exploded corn kernel is popcorn.

Popcorn: Ideally, I should have 12 -14% moisture. It takes that much moisture to create enough steam to pop the kernel.

Grower: If the corn dries out too much, there is no moisture to turn to steam. If there is no steam, there is no power inside the corn kernel to pop. If the kernel does not pop, it simply burns or only partially opens.

Historian: In 1952, Orville Redenbacher developed a hybrid popcorn that was just right to produce a large fluffy kernel. With this hybrid, almost all the kernels popped.

Consumer: When Redenbacher tried to sell us his popcorn, we didn't buy it. We thought it cost too much money.

Historian: But Redenbacher reasoned that people were willing to pay a slightly higher price if more of the kernels popped. He started his own company and proved his theory was right.

Popcorn: I've been around for many years. I am grown in almost all corners of the world.

Historian: The popularity of popcorn continues to grow. By the late 1940s, 85% of movie theaters sold popcorn.

Popcorn: I'm being raised by many popcorn growers who plant and harvest me on hundreds of acres, or on several acres as a cash crop.

Grower: Today, we raise popcorn for entrepreneurs who sell it under many brand names.

Historian: In the early 1990's, the following reports were made: The Snappy Popcorn Company, a small company in Breda, Iowa, produced 5,000,000 pounds of popcorn a year. Orville Redenbacher produced 110,000,000 pounds of popcorn a year!

Consumer: That's a lot of popcorn!

Popcorn: What is your favorite brand? What is your favorite flavor: salted, unsalted, carmel, cheese or just plain?

Consumer: The better the corn tastes and the easier it is to prepare, the more I will eat it.

Popcorn: Keep me in mind when you want a healthy snack. You honor our ancestors when you do that!

Grower: And keep our businesses thriving.

Historian: Will you be the one to develop better popcorn and find a better way to market it? Who knows?

Consumer: We'll be waiting.

Popcorn: Enjoy each and every kernel. Good-bye.   *The End*

Refreshing Beverages

Cast
> C.L. Grigg.
> Charles E. Hires.
> J.S. Pemberton
> Dr. Thomas Bramwell Welch
> Market Research Expert
> Consumer

Modifications you may wish to make
> *If your area has a soft drink manufacturing company, visit it,*
> *or ask a representative from the company to be a guest presenter.*

Brand names and/or registered trademarks referenced in this play include:
Hires Root Beer, 7-Up, Howdy Orange Drink, Welch's Grape Juice, Coca Cola, Coke.

Hires: I am Charles E. Hires. I borrowed $3,000 to start a drug store. My name is on Hires Root Beer because I started that product.

Expert: Hires was one of those people who recognized a marketable product. The first product he sold was "potter's clay."

Hires: Workmen were digging out a cellar. They were removing dirt - a special kind of dirt which I recognized as "potter's clay."

Consumer: Potter's clay removes stains from woolen garments.

Hires: My next product was root beer. Root Beer was developed from a recipe a farm wife used for making tea from many different wild roots and berries.

Expert: Some of the wild roots and berries included juniper, pipsissewa, and sarsasparilla.

Hires: I asked her for the recipe and she gave it to me. From this basic recipe I experimented until I had an extract that would produce an interesting good-tasting beverage.

Consumer: Hires Herb Tea, as he called it, was a condensed extract. The extract was mixed with exact proportions of water, sugar and yeast.

Expert: The name, Hires Herb Tea, suggests a medicine and therefore, the sales potential was limited.

Hires: The name was later changed to Hires Root Beer Extract. And my name lives on.

Consumer: Another popular soft drink is 7-Up. Mr. C.L. Grigg will describe how he developed 7-Up.

Grigg: My name is C.L.Grigg. My first successful drink was Howdy Orange Drink. It was developed in 1920.

Consumer: I bought Howdy Orange Drink every now and then.

Expert: Because Howdy Orange Drink was only moderately successful, Grigg's enterprise had to diversify. To "diversify" means to add another product, or type of product, that would appeal to the buyers.

Consumer: Grigg's second product also used the citrus fruit appeal. This time it was a combination of lemon and lime.

Grigg: The original name for 7-Up was Bib-Label Lithiated Lemon-Lime Soda. The market was mothers of infants. The advertising suggested that it would settle stomachs.

Consumer: We liked it. We bought more of it after the advertising was directed to a broader market.

Expert: Several changes of formula and many advertising campaigns continue to make 7-Up a popular consumers' item.

Consumer: Grape juice is a favorite beverage in our house. For information on Welch's Grape Juice, we welcome Dr. Thomas Bramwell Welch.

Welch: I am Dr. Thomas Bramwell Welch. You recognize my name on grape juice and jelly. I was a dentist by trade.

Expert: Dr. Thomas Bramwell Welch was a prohibitionist - a man opposed to drinking alcoholic beverages. The church he attended served wine for communion.

Welch: I wanted to be a part of the church and wanted the communion service to continue. But I thought a nonalcoholic substance should replace the wine.

Consumer: He marketed the product as Welch's Unfermented Wine. The idea was not successful.

Welch: My name could have been lost. It wasn't lost because my youngest son, Charles, thought that the marketing approach to selling the grape juice was wrong.

Expert: Charles thought that grape juice should be advertised as a healthy wholesome drink for the whole family.

Consumer: When the name of Welch's Unfermented Wine was changed to Welch's Grape Juice, I became interested. I served it to my family and friends. They liked it.

Expert: Continuous advertising has made Welch's Grape Juice a successful product.

Consumer: Thank you for that information. Mr. Pemberton, what was your contribution to the refreshing beverage market?

Pemberton: I am John S. Pemberton, a Civil War confederate veteran. I developed Coca-Cola.

Expert: After the Civil War, Pemberton went into the drug business. He was not successful. He was always experimenting.

Pemberton: Much of my experimentation was on soft drinks. In May, 1886, I finally made a mixture that satisfied me.

Expert: He didn't know what to call it. He asked his friend and bookkeeper, Mr. Robinson, for ideas.

Pemberton: F.M. Robinson suggested a name that combined two of the ingredients. "Coca" for the dried leaves of a South American plant, and "cola" for the kola nut.

Consumer: We liked it. We bought it. Coca Cola, or "Coke" is on many shopping lists today.

Expert: That completes our information on refreshing beverages and the entrepreneurs who developed and marketed them.

Consumer: The next time you buy a refreshing beverage, think about the entrepreneur who developed it.

Grigg, Hires, Pemberton, Welch:
Continue to buy our products. Good-bye.

The End

Rocky Starts

Cast
   Narrator One
   Narrator Two
   Entrepreneur
   Market Expert

Modifications you may wish to make:
   Display the products talked about in this play.
   This play offers opportunities to find out information
      about local entrepreneurs.

Brand names and/or registered trademarks referenced in this play include: Post-It Notes, Jello, Toni.

One: Today's play is about entrepreneurs and their
         efforts to be successful. Each was successful
         - but not right away. They had rocky starts.

Two: We will look at several companies and why
         each had a rocky start. We'll also review
         what corrected the rocky start.

Entrepreneur: William Wrigley, Jr. wanted to sell more
         baking powder and soap. He offered gum as a
         free premium for buying soap and baking powder.

Expert: Sales did not improve but customers did want more
         gum. Wrigley soon put aside the soap and baking
         powder and concentrated on the gum.

One: Post-It Notes were developed by the 3M Corporation
         of St. Paul, Minnesota. The company wanted to develop
         a certain kind of adhesive. The experiment didn't work.
         The new adhesive would stick to things and then could
         be easily removed.

Two: And so, Post-It Notes was born.
         Sometimes the success of a product
         is finding the right use for a failure.

© Lois F. Roets 1995

Entrepreneur: Jell-O was not an immediate success.
Peter Cooper had the patent for the gelatin.
But the general public wasn't interested.
The first entrepreneur sold it to another.

Expert: The new owner gave samples - along with a
set of directions - on how to use it. Directions
were written in French, German, Spanish, Swedish,
English, and Hebrew. Samples were also delivered
by rural postal carriers.

Entrepreneur: Jello-O became a great success. Sales grew.
By 1968, the average American family bought 16
boxes of Jello-O a year. Today it continues to sell
in boxes and in products with a gelatin base.

One: Home permanents to make your hair curly
were developed because many people could
not afford the money or the time to get a
permanent in the beauty salons.

Two: Richard Harris bought the Noma company
which produced home permanents. He tried
many different solutions.

Expert: The product and the directions on how to
give the home permanent underwent many
changes. Prices also were adjusted. A price
that is too low suggests to the customer that
a product is inferior - of little value.

Entrepreneur:Harris worked with local merchants to advertise
home permanents. The ad that drew the most
attention was "Which twin has the Toni?"

One: Because the hair of both twins looked beautiful,
the ad suggested that your hair could be made
beautiful at home as well as in the beauty salon.

Expert: Home permanents are now available from many
companies. Consumers have choices.

--- optional insert ---
Interview local merchants which describe "rocky phases"
of their business. These reports may be summarized
here. The format is:

I interviewed (name) _____ *of*

*(company)*_____. *She/he told me*

that one time the company had a "rocky time"

because _____

_____.

*The problem was solved when*_____

_____

_____.

Her/His advice to entrepreneurs is _____

_____.

Two: Thanks for being with us today as we
reviewed successful products. Each of
these products went through a "rocky time"
before becoming the success it now is.

Expert: Entrepreneurs start businesses. They are
successful if the product meets the public's
needs and the public is willing to buy it.

Historian: Will you be the next entrepreneur in your community?

One: Our play is ended.

The End

Salty Munchies

Cast
Salt
Narrator One
Narrator Two
Historian One
Historian Two
Potato Chip
Pretzel
Peanut

Modifications you may wish to make
Display other salty munchies that are enjoyed or manufactured locally.

Salt: I am salt - that distinct taste that lingers on the tongue.
I am salt - that wonderful compound that saves
      lives and preserves foods.
This play is about me, and the munchies I live with.

Historian One: Salt was once so precious that it was used
for money to pay wages.

Historian Two: Roman soldiers were paid in salt. From this
practice came the expression "To earn one's salt"
as an expression of hired labor.

Historian One: To be "Not worth his salt" means that
someone didn't do a good job.

Salt: I preserve food. I flavor food. I provide
needed elements for the body.

Narrator One: Salt is on many of our munchies -
those things we like to eat between meals, while
watching movies, and crunching at a ball game.

Narrator Two: The munchies we will talk about are
pretzels, potato chips, and peanuts.

Salt: Pretzels, potato chips and peanuts -
they are all my good friends.

Narrator One: Our first guest is Mr. (Ms. Mrs. Miss) Potato Chip.

Potato Chip:	Hello. I'm (Ms. Mrs. Miss) Potato Chip. I come in various tastes and shapes. I can be plain or ruffled, regular, onion & chives, barbecue, cheese, ranch and many other flavors.
Historian One:	The first potato chip was made by the Native American, George Crum, a chef in a resort in Saratoga Springs, New York. He tried to please a dissatisfied customer and discovered potato chips.
Historian Two:	Chef Crum had served thickly-cut potato slices and the customer didn't like them. The chef tried to satisfy the customer and made chips over and over again - each time getting the potato slices thinner and thinner. When the slices were so thin, and completely browned, the customer was satisfied.
Salt:	Potato chips weren't always as salty as they are today. However, potato chips and I have been partners for a long time.
Potato Chip:	You see, I was invented in 1853. I was so popular I was added to the menu as "Saratoga Chips." When Crum later opened his own restaurant, I was one of his featured attractions.
Historian One:	In the 1920s Herman Lay, a traveling salesman, popularized the food in the South. He sold potato chips out of the trunk of his car.
Historian Two:	Potato chips have increased in popularity every since.
Salt:	I am on potato chips. I am also on pretzels and peanuts.
Narrator One:	The pretzel is our next salty guest.
Pretzel:	I am (Ms. Mrs. Miss) Pretzel. I come in large, medium or small sizes. I can be hard or soft, very salty or not-so-salty. My texture is chewy or crunchy. I am often served with mustard.

Narrator One:	How were you invented?
Pretzel:	I was the creation of a medieval monk who gave us to children as a reward for memorizing prayers. The monk arranged the dough like folded arms - like children's arms praying.
Historian One:	The pretzel has been around since the middle ages. The shape of pretzels remained the same - even to our present day.
Historian Two:	The pretzel, like many salty munchies today, is increasing in popularity.
Pretzel:	I'm glad you like me. My history is an old history - all the way back to the middle ages. I'll probably be around for the next thousand years.
Narrator One:	Thanks for visiting us. We'll see you - with your traditionally folded arms.
Salt:	My popularity increases. As my popularity increases, entrepreneurs find more ways to make you *(motions to audience)* buy me.
Narrator Two:	Our next guest is the peanut.
Peanut:	Thanks for inviting me here today. I am Peanut. My history includes feeding people - to keep them from starving and to give them enjoyment.
Historian One:	The peanut has been around for a long time. It was in North America before Columbus arrived. However, it was not always a snack food.
Historian Two:	Many interesting facts pertain to the peanut. The peanut plant came from South America to the area we know today as Virginia.
Peanut:	I was eaten by poor people and livestock. In the Civil War, hungry soldiers ate me. It was a good thing I was there.

Historian One: Yes, indeed, you did keep many people from
                   starving. But people soon learned to enjoy you.
                   You became a food of choice - not necessity.

Peanut: P. T. Barnum, the circus organizer, promoted peanuts.

Historian Two: Peanuts were brought to China by American missionaries.
                   The Chinese developed many delicious recipes using them.

Historian One: George Washington Carver developed many uses for the
                   peanut. This made it worthwhile to raise them.

Peanut: Today I am seen everywhere. Airlines serve me in
                   little bags to their passengers. I'm in almost every
                   vending machine. I'm really very popular.

Narrator One: Today, peanuts are roasted, dry roasted, coated with salt,
                   coated with honey. They are smoked and barbecued.

Narrator Two: What will the next flavor be?

Peanut: Maybe you in the audience will give me a new
                   flavor. I welcome all new flavors so long as it
                   keeps me popular.

Historian One: Seldom has a simple plant had such a long and
                   diversified history.

Historian Two: The rest of its history is yet to be written - by us.

Narrator One: Thanks for being with us, Pretzel, Peanut and
                   Potato Chip. Your presence is always welcome.

Salt: Good-bye, my friends. See you in the supermarkets,
                   vending machines, athletic areas, and in your homes.

Potato Chip, Pretzel, Peanut: Good-bye.

The End

A Taste for the Spicy

Cast

Reader One
Reader Two
Reader Three
Reader Four
Reader Five

Modifications you may wish to make:
Reassign parts for more readers.
Make display cards for the words used in the play:

Liquamen - Roman
ke-tsiap - Chinese
kechap - Malay

Brand names and/or registered trademarks referenced in this play include:
Ketchup, Heinz Tomato Catsup, Worcester Sauce, Lea & Perrins, A.I. (Steak Sauce), Tobasco Sauce.

One: Our play is called "A Taste for the Spicy."

Two: It is about entrepreneurs who developed
condiments - spicy sauces we put on food.

Three: Ketchup is history's oldest condiment. It was
first prepared by the Romans about 300 B.C.

Four: The Roman recipe called for vinegar, oil, pepper,
and paste of dried anchovies. It was called "liquamen."
Small jars bearing the name of Liquamen were found
in the ruins of Pompeii.

Five: The next step in the history of ketchup comes
from the Chinese, who developed a tangy sauce.

One: The Chinese, like the Romans, used it on fish
and fowl. The Chinese recipe called for a brine
of pickled fish, shellfish, and spices. It was named
"ke-tsiap." In Malay, that word became "kechap."

Two: Eighteenth century British seamen brought
"kechap" back to England. English chefs
attempted to make the condiment.

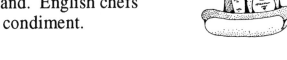

Three: They did not have the Eastern spices so they added English items such as mushrooms, walnuts and cucumbers. At this point, there were no tomatoes in it.

Four: Tomatoes come into the picture about 1790 in New England. At that time, it was proved that the tomato was not poisonous. Before that time, people thought tomatoes were poisonous.

Five: In America, Thomas Jefferson was one of the first to grow the tomato. One of his recipes was for tomato catsup.

One: Homemade tomato catsup takes much time, energy and skill. It was a relief when Henry Heinz manufactured Tomato Catsup.

Two: Heinz advertised catsup as the "Blessed relief for Mother and the other women in the household!" It was an immediate success.

Three: Henry Heinz was an energetic entrepreneur who started his company with horseradish and pickles. His first business partnership went bankrupt.

Four: His second business was more successful. Henry Heinz realized that advertising was the ticket to a successful company.

Five: He drew attention to his company at the Columbian Exposition in Chicago from 1892 to 1893.

One: The Heinz booth was out of the way on the second floor. Few people were visiting his exhibit.

Two: He quickly printed cards that said that if fairgoers would come to the Heinz booth, they would get a free pickle charm souvenir. He gave away over 1,000,000 pickle charms.

Three: Today, the Heinz Company sells pickles,
ketchup, mustard and relishes. The efforts
of Henry Heinz, the Pickle King, live on.

Four: Worcestershire Sauce is our next spicy
condiment to be reviewed. It is based on
the traditional flavors of India.

Five: Sir Marcus Sandys served as governor in India.
He liked tasty food. His cook in India had prepared
a secret blend of spices and seasonings which
Sandys liberally poured on many Indian dishes.

One: When he returned to England, he commissioned two
chemists to create a similar mixture. They did so.

Two: The product was named after Sandys's
home in Worcester, England.

Three: The chemists, John Lea and William Perrins,
secured Sandys' permission to start a company
to manufacture and market the product.

Four: It became known as Lea and Perrins Worcester Sauce.
The public liked it. The public still likes it today.

Five: A. I. Steak Sauce is another spicy taste we like. It was
created by a chef for England's King George IV.

One: The chef made a spicy condiment consisting of soy,
vinegar, anchovy and onions. It is said that the king
declared it was good, "A-1." The name stayed.

Two: Have you seen that little red bottle with hot
Tobasco Sauce? Tobasco Sauce was developed
by Edmund McIlhenny on Avery Island.

Three: Avery island is near the marshy coasts of Cajun
country in Louisiana. Avery Island has salt mines.

Four: The islanders also raise capsicum hot peppers.
         It is those hot peppers that are made into
         Tobasco Sauce - a sauce named after the
         Tobasco River in southern Mexico.

Five: Edmund McIlhenny fled to Avery Island during
         the Civil War. When the island was invaded to
         get the salt, he fled to Texas.

One: When McIlhenny returned to Avery, his home and
         crops were ruined - all except the very hot peppers.

Two: McIlhenny was a true entrepreneur who saw what was
         available and determined a way to make a profit from it.
         And it was the hot red peppers that were available.

Three: His first mixtures tasted awful. So he created new
         recipes. Finally he chopped the hot peppers and
         added them to a spicy sauce which contained
         vinegar. The mixture aged in wooden barrels.

Four: The mixture sold very well and continues to sell
         well today. When you use the fiery taste of spice
         from the little red Tobasco Sauce jar, take care
         - and use only what your taste buds will tolerate!

Five: This completes the review of several entrepreneurs
         who developed sauces, spreads, and relishes.

One: What spicy tastes do you like?

Two: Do you like to combine several spicy sauces?

Three: Do your friends like your strange mixtures?

Four: If so, you may be the next entrepreneur.

Five: Enjoy condiments - the enhancers of food.
         Enjoy the taste for the spicy.

The End

Toys

Cast
  Experimenter
  Entrepreneur
  Narrator
  Person (who played with the toy)

Modifications you may wish to make:
  Add information on other current fads - if you wish.

Brand names and/or registered trademarks referenced in this play include:
  Frisbee, Hula Hoop, Silly Putty, Slinky.

Experimenter:	Our topic today is toys - toys that have have interesting origins. Some toy ideas were new. Some were old ideas marketed in new packages. The first toy of this Readers' Theater is the Hula Hoop.
Narrator One:	In 1958, the Hula Hoop fad came to the United States. Americans bought twenty million Hula Hoops. The Hula Hoop was placed around the waist.
Person:	It's fun! You move your body in rapid rotating motions. The hoop spins and does interesting things.
Narrator Two:	Doctors didn't like this toy. They treated young and old for neck and back injuries.
Entrepreneur:	In 1958, Hula Hoops were a craze in America. But they had been around before. If you study the history of entrepreneurs and the products they marketed, you will often see an idea coming back in a slightly different form.
Narrator One:	The children in ancient Egypt and later in Greece and Rome made hoops from dried and stripped grapevines.
Narrator Two:	South American cultures devised play hoops from sugarcane plants. In the 14th century, children and adults played with wood or metal rings or hoops around their waist.

Person:	Doctors warned us of dangers. Their warnings made no difference. Twirling the hoops was fun.
Entrepreneur:	Perhaps in another 50-100 years, a different version of the Hula Hoop will become popular. Doctors will warn but few people will listen.
Person:	When something is fun, we don't always listen to reason.
Experimenter:	The second toy we'll talk about today is the Frisbee.
Narrator One:	In the 1870s, a New England confectioner, William Russell Frisbie, opened a bakery that baked homemade pies. They were baked in circular tin pans embossed with the family surname: Frisbee.
Narrator Two:	No one is certain how tossing the pans became a sport. What we do know is that by the mid 1940's, students at Yale University were tossing the pan as a game.
Narrator One:	The fad might have died out except that Walter Frederick Morrison, a man from California, became interested in the flying pans or saucers. He marketed them.
Narrator Two:	What started as a past time and relaxation became - at the hand of a marketer and entrepreneur - a national past time that has lasted for several generations.
Person:	And who knows how much longer it will last? We learned to play Frisbee when we were young. We still play it as adults. We even create our own competitions for ourselves and our dogs.
Experimenter:	Let's now turn our attention to Silly Putty.
Narrator One:	In the early 1940s, the U.S. war department wanted an inexpensive substitute for synthetic rubber. After the usual trial and error experimentation, a product emerged that was rubber-like.

Narrator Two:	However, it stretched more than rubber. It bounced 25% more than rubber. Because of these unusual qualities, it was not a good substitute for rubber. What could be done with it?
Experimenter:	In 1945, General Electric sent samples to engineers - asking for their suggestions as to what use this unusual substance could serve.
Narrator One:	The scientists did not come up with a good idea.
Narrator Two:	However, a former advertising copywriter did. His name was Paul Hodgson. Paul was now running a toy store.
Entrepreneur:	Hodgson entered into an agreement with General Electric for rights to this substance. He hired a Yale University student to separate it into one-ounce balls.
Narrator One:	Each ball was put inside a colored egg. In 1949, Silly Putty, as he called it, outsold every other item in Hodgson's toy store.
Person:	I didn't know how Silly Putty began. I just knew it was fun.
Experimenter:	Other people found other uses for the substance: pick up cat fur and lint, clean ink from fingers and paper, and other inventive uses.
Narrator Two:	In 1977, Binney & Smith acquired the rights to Silly Putty. The same peachy color was retained.
Entrepreneur:	In the 1990s, Silly Putty was celebrating fifty years of enjoyment. Binney & Smith celebrated by making Silly Putty available in new neon colors of green, blue, yellow and magenta.
Person:	In the 1990s, lots of things were painted neon colors. The colors were bright. But the best of Silly Putty is not its color but the fun you can have with it.

Entrepreneur:	As of today, the unsuccessful rubber substitute has only one commercial use - a toy. And we are happy with that result - until we get another idea. Then we'll market it!
Experimenter:	Another toy that began as serious research is the springy Slinky.
Person:	I've played with a Slinky for as long as I can remember. My friend and I raced our Slinkies. We made rules and formed a Slinky Club.
Narrator One:	In the early 1940s, marine engineer Richard James wanted to develop a spring that would reduce the motion of the waves on delicate navigating instruments.
Experimenter:	The sea continually rocks up and down and from side to side. This continuous motion in several directions causes stress to instruments on ships.
Narrator Two:	He hoped to develop a spring that could be placed under the instruments to absorb this perpetual motion. If successful, the spring would make the navigational instruments last longer and be more accurate.
Experimenter:	One day, while working in his home laboratory, he accidentally bumped the coiled spring. It fell - but not with one thud. It moved itself along from object to object as it descended to the floor.
Narrator One:	He was surprised. He tried it again and again.
Narrator Two:	Again and again it reached out and pulled itself along as it descended to the lowest level. It would even go down steps - one at a time.
Entrepreneur:	An idea is profitable only if someone can see a marketable product in it. Richard's wife looked at the coil. It looked like a great toy.

Narrator One:	Betty James, Richard's wife, was the creative thinker. She saw the coil as a marketable toy. She studied the dictionary to find a word that would describe the action of this coiled spring.
Narrator Two:	"Slinky" best described its action. "Slinky" became its name. She and her husband became entrepreneurs in 1946 to market this spring as a toy.
Person:	Slinkies have delighted many people over many years. They are fun. Their slow slinking motion is funny and interesting to watch.
Narrator One:	They also have been used as tools. In Vietnam, they were tossed over a tree branch as a quick radio antenna.
Narrator Two:	They have been on space flights to test the effects of zero gravity.
Experimenter:	Research and development of new ideas in science and toys often overlap. Who knows what will be next?
Narrator One:	One thing is certain: it takes trial and error to develop new products.
Narrator Two:	It takes a creative mind to determine a use for a failed scientific inquiry.
Entrepreneur:	After the idea has been created, it takes an entrepreneur to market it.
All:	Will your idea be the toy for the 21st century?

The End

1. *Analyzing why a product or service is successful*

Marketable product or service: *bubble gum*

Sold through (catalog, store....): *store*

Customers - those who need or want the product or service:

children, teenagers

Marketing factors that influence purchase:

✔ reasonable price   ✔ easily secured   ___ greatly needed

✔ my friends have it   ___ my life is easier with the product

✔ my life is happier with the product/service

___ it is a necessity - I have no choice

other reasons: _____

2. *Analyzing why a product or service is successful*

Marketable product or service: *baby diapers*

Sold through (catalog, store....): *stores*

Customers - those who need or want the product or service:

parents / child care workers

Marketing factors that influence purchase:

✔ reasonable price   ✔ easily secured   ✔ greatly needed

___ my friends have it   ✔ my life is easier with the product

✔ my life is happier with the product/service

✔ it is a necessity - I have no choice

other reasons: _____

3. *Analyzing why a product or service is successful*

Marketable product or service: *movie/videos*

Sold through (catalog, store....): *store, catalog*

Customers - those who need or want the product or service:

all ages and professions

Marketing factors that influence purchase:

✔ reasonable price   ✔ easily secured   ___ greatly needed

✔ my friends have it   ___ my life is easier with the product

✔ my life is happier with the product/service

___ it is a necessity - I have no choice

other reasons: _____

Analyzing Why a Product or Service is Successful

Marketable product or service: _____

Sold through (catalog, store....): _____

Customers - those who need or want the product or service:

_____

Marketing factors that influence purchase:

___ reasonable price   ___ easily secured   ___ greatly needed

___ my friends have it   ___ my life is easier with the product

___ my life is happier with the product/service

___ it is a necessity - I have no choice

other reasons: _____

Understanding Successful Entrepreneurship

<u>Entrepreneurs need:</u>

1. A product or service that is marketable
   - something consumers want or need.

Some ideas:

Needs: health, safety, food, shelter, warmth / coolness, clothes, transportation, communications, friendship, humor .....

Your ideas: _____

_____

Wants: beauty, comfort, entertainment, delight, amusement, decoration, vacation, ...

Your ideas: _____

_____

Target buyers: children, teenagers, parents, sports centers ....

Buyers for your product/service: _____

_____

2. Money (capital)
   - to start and run the business.

Some ideas: your own money, bank, friends, business partner, corporate stock, business loan, ...

Your ideas: _____

3. A marketing plan
   - to bring products/services to the consumer.

Some ideas: mail order, door-to-door, retail store, franchise, distributorships, home demonstrations, workshops ....

Your ideas: _____

Directions: Use this form - if you need a form to plan your entrepreneurship.

Planning Form for New Product or Service

My name _____   Date_____

My marketable product or service idea: _____

Customers - those who will need or want my product or service:

----

1. Marketable product or service.
Identify the needs or wants of people or society that your product or service will give.

    Needs: *Wants:*

   _____   _____

   _____   _____

   _____   _____

2. Money (capital) to start/run the business.
Identify sources of money and how the money will be used.

    Source of money: *Money needed for:*

   _____   _____

   _____   _____

   _____   _____

   _____   _____

   _____   _____

3. Marketing plan
List which marketing plan(s) you will use to bring your product to the consumers.

   Door-to-door   *Mail-order*   *Retail Store / Office*

  _____   _____   _____

  _____   _____   _____

  _____   _____   _____

  _____   _____   _____

  _____   _____   _____

  _____   _____   _____

Notes

Notes

Index
Volume Three: Entrepreneurs